Z12

AF496494

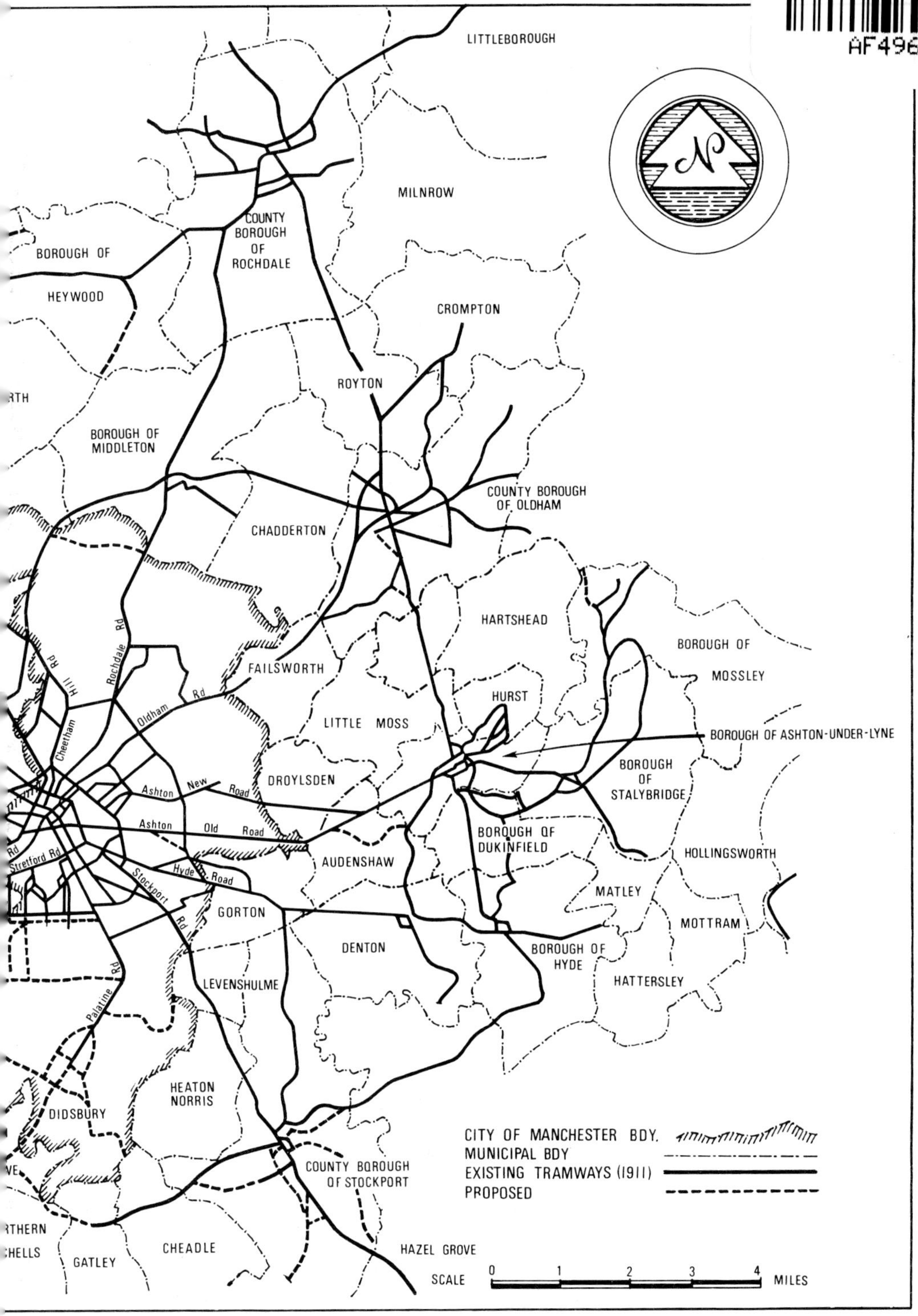

Roads & Rails
of
Manchester
1900-1950

REGAL
ALBERT SQUARE
35B
52

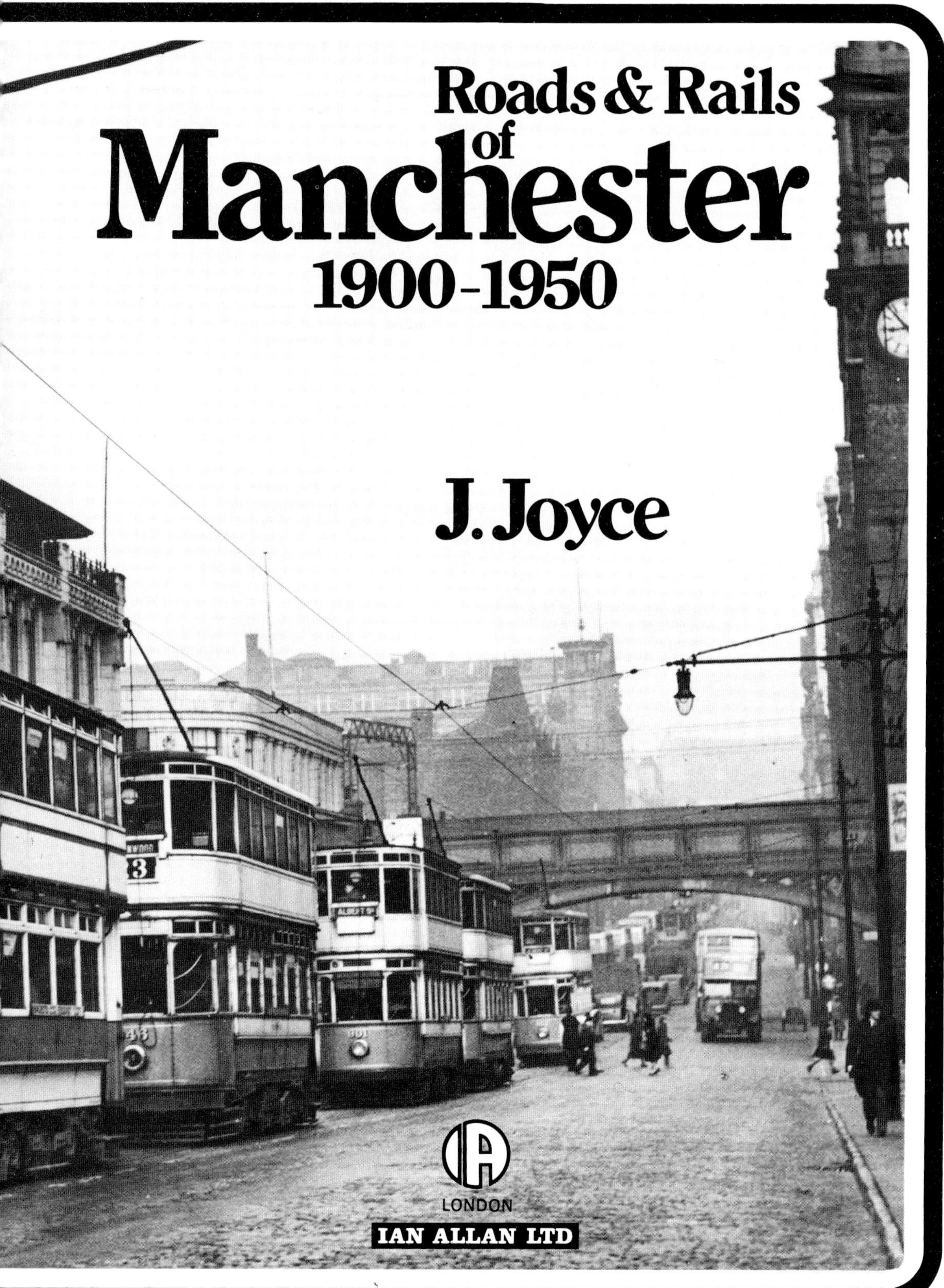

Roads & Rails
of
Manchester
1900-1950

J. Joyce

Contents

Title page: The morning rush: a line of tramcars makes its way along Oxford Road, Manchester, in 1938. *Guardian Newspapers*

This picture: The varied assortment of rolling stock visible in this 1943 view of New Barns Junction suggests the wide range of traffic handled on the Manchester Ship Canal Company's own railways. In the foreground one of the company's own locomotives is hard at work. *Manchester Ship Canal Company*

Introduction

Traditionally the Manchester region has been portrayed as a boundless wasteland of gaunt mills over-shadowing rows of terraced houses, standing in endless grey streets where tram tracks gleamed in the granite setts as one town merged imperceptibly into the next. While the heritage of industrialism lent more than enough truth to this picture, the growth of trade and prosperity which it represented was greatly dependent on the evolution of an effective transport system, from the Bridgewater Canal of 1761 to the Liverpool & Manchester Railway of 1830 and to the complex and individualistic networks of railways, tramways and bus services.

In the 18th century Manchester was described by Defoe as 'the greatest mere village in England'. Now the Greater Manchester region is one of the major conurbations of Britain; the Metropolitan County created under the Local Government Act of 1972 embraces not only the city of Manchester itself, but also neighbouring Salford and adjacent towns including Wigan, Bolton, Bury, Rochdale, Oldham, Ashton-under-Lyne, Stalybridge and Stockport. In all, the population of the county totals more than $2\frac{1}{2}$ million. Since 1969 the local passenger transport facilities of the region have been welded together into one unit, first under the South East Lancashire and North East Cheshire Passenger Transport Authority (SELNEC) and then by the Greater Manchester Passenger Transport Executive. But before this, numerous different operators — large and small, municipal and company — presented a variegated pattern of services within and between their respective terrains.

The object of this book is to look back into this period and examine some of the themes which underlay transport development in the Greater Manchester region, particularly during the years between 1900 and 1950, the half century in which the public transport system reached its zenith. These were the years when electric tramways brought a new mobility to the ordinary townsfolk; municipal enterprise flourished as smartly-appointed cars wearing their town's livery and coat of arms reflected local pride and established the concept of transport's social role in the community. Yet while a strong corporate tradition grew up, widespread cooperation and the idea of a regional transport authority foreshadowed later steps towards integration. It was also a period of drastic change;

within a few short years the tramcar was being superseded by the motor bus, which opened up new vistas of suburb and countryside, while fundamental economic and social changes affected the transport pattern. The distribution of population altered as the residential area extended southward into Cheshire and population declined in the older inner districts, while the staple textile industry was eclipsed as new industries emerged. And all the time there were persistent problems such as the struggle against congestion, the controversy over integration of both road and rail operations, and the need for investment in new facilities; all these issues are still relevant to present-day conditions.

This book is by no means a comprehensive history; nor can it claim to be a work of original scholarship. It is no more than an illustrated compilation which attempts to highlight a few aspects of the past transport scene in a particular area. I hope that it may prove to be of some interest to those who regard Greater Manchester as a very special part of the world and who may recall something of the period concerned, and that it may serve as a modest reminder of the crucial role played by local transport in the evolution of a great conurbation.

My debts are obvious. I am especially indebted to those who have chronicled the transport history of the area and have published the results of their labours for the benefit of us all; some of their works are listed in the bibliography for the reader who may wish to look further into any aspect of the subject. I am also grateful to John Prigmore of Imperial College and to the Librarian of the Lyon Playfair Library of Imperial College for putting at my disposal the facilities of the library. I am indebted to the photographers who have generously made their own collections available to me; in particular my thanks go to G. H. F. Atkins, Roy Brook, W. A. Camwell and C. Carter, who have gone to considerable trouble to provide relevant illustrations; to John Parke and the Ian Allan Library for the use of photographs from the library, to Greater Manchester Transport, City of Manchester Local History Library, and the Port of Manchester. Not least, I am grateful to the now anonymous photographers of the past who have left us pictures of what they saw and so have enabled us to recreate an image of a bygone age.

1
The Making of a Conurbation

The age of bad roads

Our school textbooks used to tell us that Manchester was the centre of the cotton trade and one of the principal cities of Britain, its fame and fortune dependent on the growth of the textile industry. This was Macaulay's 'wonderful emporium' which, he explained, in the middle of the 17th century was 'a mean and ill-built market town' of fewer than 6,000 people, so lacking in affluence that not a single person owned a coach. By his own time, such was the increase in prosperity that there were 20 coachmakers in Manchester.

Transport played a crucial role in the development of an area that made industrial England the 'workshop of the world' in the 19th century. It was the needs of industry that called forth improvements in transport facilities to cope with the increasing demand for better and faster movement of both raw materials and the products of industry. The Manchester region was well to the fore in the latest transport modes, from canals to the first of the modern railways. And as the city grew, together with the towns around it that now form the Greater Manchester County, so internal transport services had to be provided, leading to the growth of tramway and omnibus networks.

Bad roads have been a constant cause of complaint for centuries, and Lancashire in the Industrial Revolution does not seem to have been above the national average. A favourite quotation from the short section of the history textbook devoted to transport recalled that indefatigable traveller Arthur Young, who journeyed through England during the 1770s and recorded his impressions; this is what he said about the road to Wigan:

'I know not in the whole range of language terms sufficiently expressive to describe this infernal road. Let me most seriously caution all travellers who may accidentally propose to travel this terrible country to avoid it as they would the devil. They will here meet with ruts which I actually measured four feet deep, and

floating with mud only from a wet summer. What therefore must it be after a winter? The only mending it receives is the tumbling in of some loose stones, which serve no other purpose but jolting a carriage in the most intolerable manner'.

This was not the only travel problem that Young encountered, but since he seems to have been an inveterate grumbler, perhaps it may be assumed that not all roads were such hard going. Certainly it was possible to use some roads in safety, and the spread of the turnpike system in the 18th century led to marked improvement. The turnpike trusts were set up to undertake work on sections of highway, improving and keeping them in repair, and taking tolls from travellers passing along the roads in order to pay for the work. However, such was the growth in traffic with the rise of industry that the turnpikes were not always able to keep pace in maintaining the roads in a suitable condition to carry the growing loads. In his *Description of the Country for Thirty or Forty Miles Round Manchester* in 1795, Dr Aikin discovered in the Parish of Eccles that 'although much labour and very great expense of money' had been spent on the roads 'they still remained in an indifferent state owing to immoderate weights drawn in wagons and carts'.

Such had been the state of many roads that much traffic was not handled in wheeled vehicles at all, but was carried on packhorses. Strings of packhorses, each with its load slung on its back, were a common sight on the highways of the region. Aikin goes on to describe the method of distribution adopted by Manchester traders; the merchants would keep large numbers of packhorses, and would take them around the major towns of the area carrying their goods in the packs. They would display their wares to the shopkeepers of the town and thus sell them. Then on the way back, the horses would be loaded again with wool bought on the journey, and this in turn was brought back into Manchester to be sold to the manufacturers in the city and the surrounding towns.

Improvements made in the roads during the turnpike era were sufficient to allow this method of working to be changed. Instead of the convoys of packhorses, wagons were put on the roads to carry the goods, while the traders themselves only rode out for the orders, taking with them their pattern books and sending on the goods afterwards by wagon. At the same time better roads permitted the traders' field of operations to be much widened, so that they could further expand their markets into other parts of the country.

As to passenger travel, the normal method was on horseback, provided you had a horse; otherwise you had to walk. By the middle of the 18th century, however, the growing town of Manchester felt the need for better communications to facilitate its trade, and in 1754 several merchants banded together to set up a 'Flying Coach' to London. The notice advertising this innovation has become one of the classics of transport ephemera:

'Incredible as it may appear, this coach will actually arrive (barring accidents) in London $4\frac{1}{2}$ days after leaving Manchester.'

More marvels were to come, for in 1760 there was a coach performing even greater feats of speed, travelling to London in only three days, an indication not only of the effects of road improvement, but of the stimulus of competition leading to the start of organised long-distance road travel. Nevertheless, if you wanted to go from Manchester to Liverpool, this still took all day and the coach ran on only three days a week; you left Manchester at six in the morning, had breakfast at Irlam, dinner at Warrington, tea at Prescot, and reached Liverpool by night.

The poorer traveller could take a place on Matthew Pickford's 'Flying Wagon' which by 1777 was running between Manchester and London in $4\frac{1}{2}$ days, carrying a mixed load of freight and passengers. Pickford seems to have been one of the earliest regular carriers, but the transport business flourished and by the early years of the 19th century many carriers were plying the roads of Lancashire. Ashton's *'Manchester Guide'* of 1804, for example, records that as many as 120 carriers were engaged in conveying goods from Manchester to all parts of the country.

Improvements in roads and in the organisation of transport led to a speeding up of travel, and by the time the road coach reached its zenith in the 1830s it was possible to journey between Manchester and London in 18 hours, at an average speed of over 10 miles an hour. One of the most famous of the coaches was Sherman's *Telegraph*; leaving London at five in the morning, it made only two 20min stops for meals on the way, while it changed horses 18 times, arriving in Manchester at eleven at night. Departure from Manchester was at a similarly early hour. Other notable coaches included the *Red Rover*, which took 20hr, and the *Royal Defiance* which took a similar time but journeyed overnight, so that by leaving Manchester at six in the evening you could be in London by the early afternoon of the following day.

Below: Hazards of road travel: the Manchester mail coach snowbound in the Derbyshire hills.

Compared with the $4\frac{1}{2}$ days of some 60 years earlier, travelling time was reduced to about one quarter.

This acceleration reflected the consuming urge for speed in commerce; the busy Manchester merchant was no longer satisfied with the old leisurely ways. The Victorian adage that 'time is money' seems to have had its origins well before the Victorian era when it took hold of the businessman and in turn encouraged better travel facilities.

Such facilities revolutionised travelling for the small number of people who could afford to ride the coach along the main highways, but there was still need for better transport for the conveyance of the bulky goods for industry. Packhorse and wagon were still costly modes of carriage, and the advance of industry depended on more economical methods of conveying heavy goods to and from the Manchester area: the coal needed for the new steam power, the imported cotton for the textile industry, and the finished goods for export to the markets of the world. Some Manchester products for export were sent via Bristol,

being transhipped at Bewdley and Bridgnorth, to which places they were carried by packhorses as well as by cumbersome wagons fitted with extra-broad wheels to prevent them sinking into the mud on the roads; the cost of transport by this means was quoted as more than £3 a ton, which amounted to a heavy burden on the trade.

Difficulty and high cost of transport also affected the growth of towns. Rapidly increasing in size and population, the industrial towns faced difficulty in obtaining sufficient food for their people. In winter when roads became impassable, Manchester was said to be like a 'beleaguered city'; the poor land around the city meant that not enough food could be produced for its growing population, which was dependent on outside sources for its supplies. But such produce as fruit and vegetables had to be carried in from considerable distances, making them scarce and expensive. Even in summer, the high cost of transport put the price of many items of food beyond the reach of most people.

Right and below: The Manchester to London coach negotiates a steep gradient in the Peak District; the journey was cut from four days in the middle of the eighteenth century to 18hr by the 1830s. By contrast, the new electric trains of the 1960s were covering the ground in $2\frac{1}{2}$hr. *Lower: R. Brook*

Transport and urban growth

'We have beautiful hill country which, a hundred years ago chiefly swamp land thinly populated, is now sown with towns and villages, and is the most densely populated strip of country in England.'

Frederick Engels, *The Condition of the Working Class in England in 1844*

A better form of bulk transport was essential to both industry and the increasing urban population; this came with the canals, a mode of transport in which the Manchester region was among the pioneers. The canal age is often said to have begun with the Sankey Brook where the existing river was improved in 1757, but the modern canal era opened with the Bridgewater Canal in 1761. For the first time this brought into use a new waterway quite separate from an existing river. Its originator was the Duke of Bridgewater who wanted a cheap method of conveying coal from his mines at Worsley into the city of Manchester where this fuel was needed to power the steam engines of industry. He employed the engineer James Brindley to construct the canal, which became world famous for its underground waterways into the mines themselves as well as the aqueduct at Barton where the canal was carried over the river. The canal was later extended to give communication with Liverpool, to provide a means of conveyance superior in economy and reliability to either river or land transit.

Effects of the canals were immediately apparent. Writing in 1805 in his book[1] on *Inland Navigation* John Phillips states:

'Before the Duke began his canal, the price of water carriage by the old navigation on the Mersey and Irwell from Liverpool to Manchester was 12s per ton, and from Warrington to Manchester 10s. Land carriage was 40s per ton. Coals were retailed to the port at Manchester at 7d per hundredweight, and often dearer. The Duke by this navigation from Liverpool to Manchester carries for only 6s per ton, in a shorter time, and as certain delivery as by land carriage; consequently one half is saved to the public of the old water carriage, and to the poor for coals, and almost six parts in seven of land carriage.'

This reduction in the cost of transport was crucial to both industry and population. The canals stimulated the widespread industrialisation of the region, especially by enabling industry to obtain cheap raw materials, notably coal. On the Manchester, Bolton & Bury Canal, opened in 1805, Phillips comments that it

Below: The Bridgewater Canal, built to convey coal to Manchester industry, started a revolution in transport in the eighteenth century. This early twentieth century view of the canal at Barton shows coal as still a prominent cargo. *R. Brook*

'opened a cheap and easy communication, not only to these towns, but also highly convenient for the inter-mediate country, which abounds with mines of coal and other minerals, in great request at Manchester'.

Other waterways included the Rochdale Canal, opened in 1804, and the Manchester and Oldham Canal, which 'commences on the east side of Manchester near a street called Piccadilly'. Both brought futher development to the country they served; in the words of Phillips, 'the country all round abounds with manufactures and manufacturers, who like a swarm of bees are continually employed by the merchants who, with a ready conveyance to the four great sea ports, diffuse these productions over the whole globe'. In 1811 the Huddersfield Canal provided a connection across the Pennines into the West Riding of Yorkshire. Thus Manchester obtained com-munication by inland waterway to the major parts of England, giving access to raw materials and markets, as well as enabling food supplies to be brought into the towns. Along the canals also travelled migrant families from other areas to swell the numbers in the towns as they sought work in thriving industry. But the canals were not long to retain their dominance.

'In September 1830 the beginning of a commercial rev-olution came in the opening of the Liverpool & Manchester Railway. A new system of travelling was thus established, which has not only served the purposes of business in a marvellous way, but has given new zest, charm, interest and range to life, thought and intercourse by bringing within cheap and easy reach the persons and the places formerly to be seen only by long, comfortless and costly journeys'.

Thus Edgar Sanderson, in his school textbook *History of the British Empire* in 1876, reminds us of the new form of transport which overtook the canals and in which the Manchester region again took a prominent part.

The Liverpool & Manchester Railway was born of dissatisfaction with waterway transport between the two cities. Despite the improvements which the navigations had brought, it was now claimed that their charges were exorbitant, that there were long delays in the carriage and delivery of goods, and that the canal companies were unwilling to make efforts to increase the traffic they handled. As the prospectus of the railway put it in 1824:

'It is not that the water companies have not been able to carry goods on reasonable terms, but that, strong in the enjoyment of their monopoly, they have not thought proper to do so. Against the most arbitrary exactions the public have hitherto had no protection, and against the indefinite continuance and recurrence of this evil they have but one security. It is compe-tition that is wanted . . .'

Competition was what the Liverpool and Manchester Railway was designed to provide. It was opened on 15 September 1830, the great occasion being described for us by Samuel Smiles in his *Life of George Stephen-son*:

'As the trains approached Manchester, crowds of people were found covering the banks, the slopes of the cuttings, and even the railway itself. The mul-titudes, become impatient and excited by the rumours which reached them, had outflanked the military, and all order was at an end. The people clambered about the carriages, holding on by the door handles, and many were tumbled over . . . On the following morning, the railway was opened for public traffic. The first train of 140 passengers was booked and sent on to Manchester, reaching it in the allotted time of two hours, and from that time the traffic has regularly proceeded from day to day until now'.

The railway's success, says Smiles, was 'complete and decisive'. Some anticipations, however, proved at fault; the railway's promoters had based their calcula-tions almost entirely on the carriage of heavy freight traffic, notably coal, cotton and timber, and little account was paid to passengers. As it turned out, the receipts obtained from passenger traffic far exceeded those derived from freight, which for a time remained a comparatively small part of the total business. The railway was expected to obtain about half of the total number of passengers which the road coaches had been carrying; that is, about 400 a day. But even in its early days the railway was handling an average of about 1,200 passengers daily, while only five years after the opening it was carrying nearly half a million passengers a year.

More railways soon followed. In 1837 the Grand Junction gave a connection with Birmingham, and then with the opening of the London & Birmingham in 1838 London could be reached in about eleven hours. However, this was a somewhat roundabout way between Cottonopolis and Metropolis, and accord-ingly the Manchester & Birmingham Railway was launched to provide a more direct route; the first section, from Manchester to Stockport (Heaton Norris), was opened on 4 June 1840, but it was another year before the famous viaduct spanning the

Above right and right: The new landscape of the railway: the Liverpool & Manchester Railway strides across the Sankey Valley and into Manchester.

Mersey at Stockport was completed to enable trains to proceed further. From Stockport to Sandbach was opened on 10 May 1842, when the new permanent station at London Road, Manchester, was also brought into use, while the final section from Sandbach to Crewe was opened on 10 August, thus making connection with the Grand Junction and completing the more direct route to London.

Meanwhile to the east of Manchester, the Manchester & Leeds Railway had been built. From Manchester as far as Littleborough was opened on 4 July 1839 and the railway was completed through to Leeds on 1 March 1841. Through rail communication across Manchester from east to west was made possible in 1844 with the connection between the Liverpool & Manchester Railway and Manchester & Leeds Railway. From 1 January the Manchester & Leeds brought into use the new Hunts Bank station, at the same time closing its original terminus at Oldham Road which was then used for goods only. The Liverpool & Manchester opened its new line from Ordsall Lane into Hunts Bank on 4 May, from which date the old Liverpool Road terminus was relegated to goods. Hunts Bank station, described at the time as 'a magnificent work', achieved distinction as the regally named 'Victoria'.

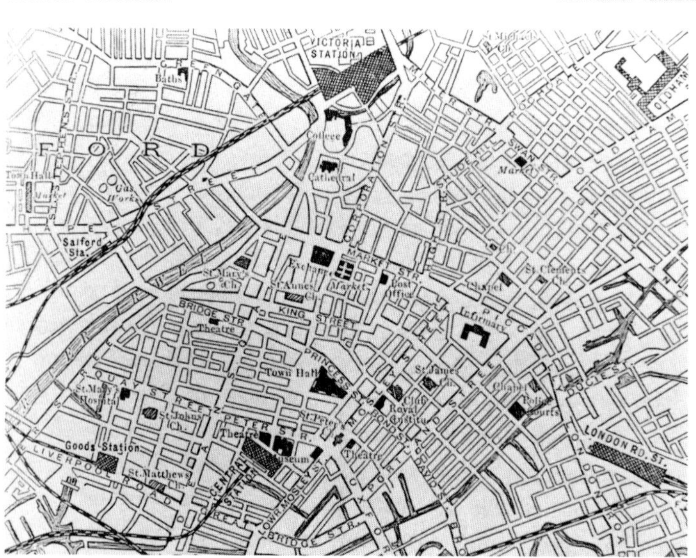

Above: Railway rivalry sometimes became heated: construction gangs of competing railways dispute the right of way at Clifton Junction in the 1840s.

Left: The railways encircle Manchester: this contemporary map of central Manchester in the 1880s shows the principal stations and the lack of communication across the city. Liverpool Road (the old Liverpool & Manchester Railway station) is at the bottom left corner, with the new Central nearby; top right is Oldham Road goods station, with London Road lower right. Victoria is prominent at the top, but Exchange has not yet been built.

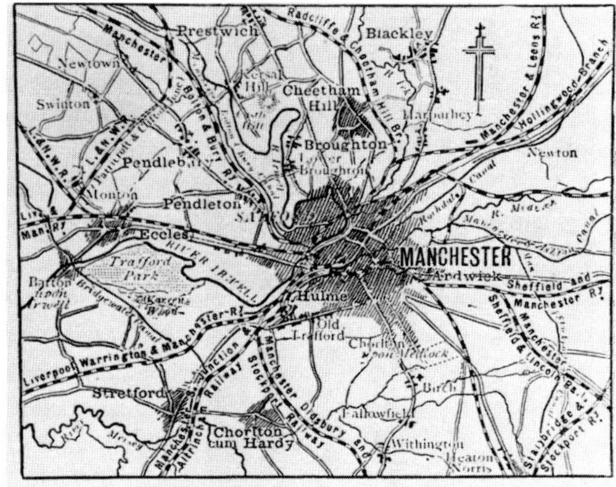

Left: The environs of Manchester about 1880. Trafford Park is still a park, while Fallowfield and Withington are rural suburbs.

Another line across the Pennines was also built in the 1840s. The first section of the Sheffield, Ashton-under-Lyne & Manchester Railway (usually simply called the Sheffield Line), was opened on 17 November 1841 from Manchester to Godley. Ashton was served by a station called Ashton & Hooley Hill. It was extended to Broadbottom (Mottram) on 10 December 1842, to Dinting on 24 December 1842, and to Hadfield and Woodhead on 8 August 1844, while the Glossop branch was opened on 9 June 1845. The line throughout was formally opened on 22 December 1845 with public services starting the following day, on the same day that the Stalybridge branch was brought into use. There was a new station at Ashton on the branch, the former one on the main line being renamed Guide Bridge.

The year 1847 saw the introduction of a name that was to achieve a particular meaning as the area's 'own' railway. An amalgamation of the Leeds & Manchester, the local Manchester, Bolton & Bury and other lines created the Lancashire & Yorkshire Railway, a title to remain familiar until the start of the 1920s.

During the railway age the population of the Manchester region grew rapidly. Manchester itself increased from some 70,000 people in 1801 to over 300,000 in 1851 and to almost 650,000 in 1901; Salford expanded from 14,000 in 1801 to over 60,000 in 1851 and to over 220,000 in 1901. Similar increases were taking place in the ring of towns which surrounded Manchester: Wigan (an important centre for the coal industry), Bolton, Bury, Rochdale, Oldham (the major cotton spinning town), Ashton-under-Lyne, Hyde, and Stockport. The principal trade, of course, was the cotton textile industry, and this was supported by an engineering industry and coal mining.

As a result, the built-up area was speedily taking over from open country, as houses and mills replaced fields and woods. The process is graphically described in the compendious *Our Own Country* in its account of Manchester in 1880:

'Expanding from the nucleus of the old town on the banks of the Irwell and the Medlock, it has incorporated into itself village after village, and pushed out further and further into the surrounding fields. Clusters of chimney stacks have replaced groves of trees; bricks and mortar are found instead of corn and hay; and many a spot which, in the memory of men now living, was a quiet country nook, is covered with busy streets.'

Such was the expansion that one town was merging into the next, creating what a later age has termed a 'conurbation'. This process was already apparent by the middle of the 19th century. In his description of the Manchester conurbation, T. W. Freeman points out that the map of 1848 reveals that 'there was already continuous building along the seven miles of road from Manchester to Oldham, and the towns of Stalybridge, Dukinfield and Ashton had fused by the spread of houses and factories between them'.

Means of local transport were essential to maintain movement within this vast densely-populated area. The great mass of the people were still obliged to live near their place of employment, and it was the more affluent folk who were able to enjoy the amenities of transport, either on horseback or in their own coaches, commuting daily between home and office. Already by the 1820s suburban traffic flows were developing, as villages such as Didsbury became popular retreats for the Manchester businessman. Short-distance coach services brought passengers into the city; Alan Bates' *Directory of Stage Coach Services 1836* shows that in this year there were about 40 coaches a day between Manchester and Stockport, and some 10 or 12 a day between Manchester, and Rochdale, Bury and Ashton.

Facilities gradually filtered down the social scale as omnibuses came on the roads to offer cheaper services with higher capacity. By the early 1820s omnibuses were operating to Manchester suburbs such as Ardwick, Broughton, Cheetham Hill and Pendleton; in 1844 Frederick Engels remarked on the middle classes residing on such 'breezy heights' with their omnibus to the city every quarter of an hour. Growing demand for such services led to severe competition among operators, and it was as a result of this that a number

15

of omnibus proprietors cooperated to form the Manchester Carriage Company in 1865.

On 17 May 1877 the first tramway in the area was opened under the auspices of the Manchester Suburban Tramways Company. This was later acquired by the Manchester Carriage company, which subsequently changed its name to the Manchester Carriage & Tramways Company to reflect its expanding interest in the new mode of transport. The company grew to become much more extensive in its sphere of influence than its title might have suggested. As well as serving Manchester itself, it also operated routes into Salford, Pendleton, Swinton and Peel Green; to Stretford and Old Trafford; to Denton, and to the neighbouring towns of Oldham, Ashton, Stalybridge and Stockport. At the height of its glory in the 1890s its services covered some 140 miles of routes, employing 500 cars, and transcending local boundaries to provide what was effectively an area transport network. Around the turn of the century this was to be drastically changed with the advent of municipally-operated electric tramways which inaugurated a new era in urban travel.

Above: The attractions of urban life: patrons gather for a Hallé concert at Manchester Free Trade Hall. The wealthy come on horseback, the majority walk.

Below: Town traffic increases: private carriages are numerous, but most people still walk, although the omnibus has now appeared. A scene at Manchester Royal Exchange in the 1880s.

2
Railways into Manchester

Railway rivalry

The Railway Magazine, 1912

Manchester's first rail connection to the south and London, made by the Grand Junction and the London & Birmingham, was followed by the shorter route between Manchester and Crewe, and both of these became amalgamated into the London & North Western Railway, which held a monopoly in this traffic into the 1850s. Then, however, other companies sought to obtain a share in what appeared to be a lucrative traffic between Cottonopolis and Metropolis. As they attempted to get their own routes to Manchester, the story became one of competition between several rival companies, resulting in a lively service for Mancunians. Competition also raged on another important route, between Manchester and Liverpool, where the pioneer railway was joined by other lines between the two cities. Consequently, rivalry ensured an abundance (even an over-abundance) of trains, and provided Manchester with some of the best train services in Britain.

An era opened in 1857 when the Manchester, Sheffield & Linconshire Railway and the Great Northern entered into an alliance to operate a service between Manchester and London. Although the LNWR had for long tried to prevent such an alliance, which was an obvious threat to its monopoly, the construction of the Great Northern route revealed new possibilities, and a 50 year agreement was signed in 1860 between the GNR and the MSLR. The new allies had a harder route between the two cities, but nevertheless their 'Manchester Fliers' succeeded in taking away a profitable part of the traffic from the LNWR and in building up a reputation for punctuality and reliability.

Through trains between Manchester and London began to be worked jointly by the GNR and MSL from 1 August 1857; the MSL handled the trains for its part of the route to Sheffield, where the GNR took them to Retford and over its main line to Kings Cross. The GNR had been given access to Sheffield in return for allowing MSL trains to enter Lincoln. Time for the fastest train was at first 5hr 20min, the same as on the shorter LNWR route. In reply the LNWR cut its

Left: 'London Road takes one far away to that outer world where the only termini are the oceans' (*The Railway Magazine*, 1901). An LNWR express prepares to depart from Manchester London Road, headed by a 'Precursor' 4-4-0. The LNWR shared the station (not always amicably) with the Great Central, whose trains can be seen to the right. *Ian Allan Library*

Above right: Railway rivalry as expressed in Edwardian posters. The LNWR boldly let the facts speak for themselves; proud of its new 'London extension', the Great Central presented its line to Manchester as 'the most comfortable and picturesque route to the North'.

timings until its best trains were down to 4hr 40min, while the GNR/MSL partners reduced theirs to 5hr. But the allies were not content with this, and gradually they cut their times down to under 5hr: to 4hr 55min, to 4hr 30min, and then by 1884 to 4hr 15min.

Cheap fares and excursions were offered, including London and back for 5s (25p) in 1858, while other and more violent methods ensued. The MSL/GN trains used the MSL's side of London Road station, and the LNW on the other side of the station entered on a regime of harassment of any travellers who had the audacity to try to enter Manchester by means of the MSL trains. One old lady was reported to have been 'frightened out of her wits', but the LNW seems to have met its match when it attempted to intimidate a lawyer, who brought his legal expertise to bear on the company. Though this apparently ended such troublesome tactics, the situation was obviously unsatisfactory to the two partners, and accordingly the MSL constructed a new line into a temporary terminus, named Manchester Central, which was opened on 2 July 1877, followed by a new permanent station opened on 1 July 1880.

Another contender for Manchester's traffic to the south was the Midland Railway. Originally the Midland's expresses used the MSL side of London Road, but in 1881 a new line was opened from Heaton Mersey Junction to Throstle Nest Junction on the Cheshire Lines, so that MR trains could work into Central. From 1888 the Midland's Manchester-London services were speeded up, including a new train leaving London St Pancras at 2pm and reaching Manchester at 6.20, making it the fastest train on the company's rails. By the end of the century the time was trimmed down to 4hr 15min, equal to that of the LNW. The Midland service established a reputation for smart working as well as comfort, while the route through the Peak District, though harder than the LNW main line, was preferred by many travellers for its scenic delights.

Changes in the competitive situation came by the turn of the century when the MSL realised its ambition to have its own line to London and became the Great Central Railway. On 15 March 1899 the newly created Great Central started a train service between Manchester London Road and London, over its new extension into its London terminus at Marylebone. Not unnaturally, the Great Northern had opposed the MSL's expansion, as it would of course affect its own services, but it gave way on being promised running powers over the Great Central for its trains into Manchester, and thereafter it worked a Manchester-London service on its own. But this was the end of cooperation between the two former partners, which for the next few years became rivals for the inter-city traffic, until, seeing the folly of competition in the face of the opposing services of the LNW and the Midland, in 1907 they proposed a working agreement which would effectively have made them into one organisation. Although this agreement was not approved by the Railway Commissioners, the two companies thereafter continued to work together more harmoniously, though by this time the heyday of the Great Northern's Manchester-London expresses was over.

After the Grouping of 1923, two of the rivals came under common management as part of the LMS, which concentrated its efforts on the former LNWR route, the old Midland line being decelerated to give a more adequate service to the cities of the Midlands rather than Manchester. It was not until the big speed-up that took place during the 1930s with the advent of larger engines that the Midland route was again accelerated and developed to take some of the increasing load from the LNW main line. At the same time, under the LNER the competition from the old Great Central remained, though this route never regained the outstanding position achieved by the former MSL and

GNR in earlier days. The fastest trains on the rival routes over the years make an interesting comparison:

Fastest trains between Manchester and London

	Distance (miles)	1897 hr	1897 min	1910 hr	1910 min	1928 hr	1928 min	1937 hr	1937 min
LNWR	189	4	15	3	30	3	30	3	15
Midland	190	4	20	3	30	4	00	3	35
GNR	209	4	15	-	-	-	-	-	-
GCR	206	-	-	4	00	4	23	4	05

Rival companies also engaged in competition over different routes between Manchester and Liverpool, resulting in a combined service which was acknowledged as one of the best in Britain in point of frequency, punctuality and speed.

First in the field of course was the Liverpool & Manchester, which became part of the LNWR, while a rival route, longer by several miles, was built by the Lancashire & Yorkshire. The situation was further complicated when in 1875 the Cheshire Lines (in which the GNR, MSL and Midland were all interested) opened a new line between the two cities, putting on trains that made the journey in 45min although the distance was greater than on the LNW. To retain its lead the LNW had to speed up its own service, with results that impressed Foxwell and Farrer to write in their compilation *Express Trains* in the 1880s that 'this bit of Lancashire ground' was 'the focus of the smartest running in the world'. They went on to describe the trains of the two rivals:
'At each even hour the North Western express starts from either end, and the Cheshire Lines at each half past, besides which 10 other trains are thrown in that do the trip in 40 minutes without a stop. There are 60 (28 London and North Western, and 32 Cheshire

Lines) of these express journeys every day, the average time being slightly over 44½ minutes'.

In addition, there were the Lancashire & Yorkshire trains, which only missed coming into Foxwell's

Below left: The Lancashire & Yorkshire Aspinall 4-4-0s with 7ft 3in driving wheels were to be seen in Manchester on the through Liverpool-Leeds expresses, as well as on trains to Blackpool. No 1105 of 1891 is here in its rebuilt form with superheater in 1909.
Ian Allan Library

Above: Pride of the Lancashire & Yorkshire were the 'Highfliers', the 40 big Atlantics constructed between 1899 and 1902. When first built No 1400 was allocated to Newton Heath for working trains from Manchester to Blackpool, Southport, Liverpool and York.
Ian Allan Library

Below: The long sloping approach road to the LNWR's London Road station gave an added dignity to its elevated situation, even if it tested the stamina of the late-coming passenger! A line of horse-drawn cabs awaits intending patrons in this Edwardian view.
R. Brook

'express' category because of the stops they made. Nevertheless, their route was still 'bustling with speed'. Nor was this an easy racing ground: 'this swarm of rapid trains have to cut their way through a maze of murky junctions, but they are as punctual as chronometers'. Indeed, the CLC in particular gained a reputation as 'the punctual service'.

The position had been transformed in 1888 when the LYR improved its route. The old way via Bolton and Wigan was nearly 40 miles, and E. L. Ahrons tells us 'no traveller from either city bothered to use it unless he had some time on his hands and specially wanted to see the verdant dales and picturesque glens of the Wigan district'. The new line between Pendleton Junction and Hindley, as well as a loop by-passing Wigan, not only reduced the route by three miles but made it easier to negotiate. Thus inspired, the Lancashire & Yorkshire, too long regarded as unimpressive in matters of rapid travel, put on a service of 45-minute expresses between Manchester and Liverpool. In addition some of these trains made the journey in 40 minutes and were extended through to Leeds, to give a useful cross-country link.

The Manchester stations from which these various services operated each had a character of its own.

Premier place could be claimed by London Road, terminus of the London & North Western's London expresses. It also housed platforms for the Great Central, and its predecessor, the Manchester Sheffield & Lincolnshire Railway, and relations between the two companies were not always of the most cordial. In 1879 an addition was made to London Road in order to accommodate the Manchester, South Junction & Altrincham Railway's trains which were then extended through from their station at Oxford Road. Later, increasing traffic, especially of a suburban nature, called for the construction of the new Mayfield station, opened on 8 August 1910; though this mainly handled local services, it was also used for some long-distance trains, especially in the summer peak, and it was unfortunate for any last-minute passenger arriving at London Road and finding that his train was due to depart from Mayfield!

One type of traffic which has long since disappeared from the station platform but which was characteristic of the heyday of the railway, was the milk traffic handled at London Road, a reminder of the part played by the railways in bringing in the food supplies that were vital to the life of the big city. About 1,200 churns a day would be brought in by train from the farms of Cheshire, Derbyshire and Staffordshire, requiring that one platform be almost entirely devoted

to this traffic. A constant succession of milk floats would be in and out of the station, returning the empties and taking away the incoming churns for distribution in the city.

At its peak, the LNWR station would be dealing with about 40,000 passengers a day, both long-distance and suburban, while business could also be intensified by the addition of excursions. Situated at the top of its lengthy approach road, the station had dignity as well as bustle, and perhaps this prompted a later age to give it the new name of 'Piccadilly' under which it has been known since 1960.

Beyond London Road, Piccadilly and Market Street, stands Victoria station, focus for services to west, north and east of Manchester. Opened in 1844, Victoria was then claimed as the largest station in England, but traffic soon outgrew the original facilities so that a new station had to be built and this was opened on 1 May 1884. By the start of the 20th century, as the headquarters of the Lancashire & Yorkshire Railway, Victoria was dealing with some 700 trains daily, conveying about 40,000 passengers, and further rebuilding was under way in 1903. Eventually the 17 platforms, together with the offices, occupying an area of nearly 15 acres, and the total length of the platforms (9,420 feet), added up to one of the largest and busiest stations in Britain. Here were trains to Yorkshire and Scotland, to Liverpool, Southport and Blackpool, as well as local services to Bolton and Blackburn, Bury, Oldham and Rochdale, and the whole of the busy industrial region of Lancashire.

A novel feature of Victoria which ensured it a place in every boy's book of railways was the overhead railway installed by the LYR in 1899 to deal with the large amount of luggage. Tracks were constructed

across the width of the station at roof level, and suspended on these ran an electric trolley, fitted with a control position for the operator and carrying an enormous basket which could be lowered to each platform and then raised again for the journey to the next platform.

Within the station confines a special siding was used by banking engines employed to give westbound trains a helping push up the bank, and it was common to see three or four engines of varying classes awaiting this duty. Ahrons tells the story, dating from earlier days when some LYR motive power was not all it might have been, of a banking engine which, having set off on its task, returned sooner than expected, the driver explaining that he had been unable to keep up with the train.

Perhaps the most unusual feature of Victoria was that another company's trains had to run through the middle of the station in order to get into their own station. This was the next-door Exchange, which had also been opened in 1884, when the LNWR trains were then transferred away from the old Victoria. LNWR trains to and from the east therefore had to traverse the length of Victoria station when entering or leaving their own Exchange. To compound the peculiarity, a continuous platform was constructed connecting the two stations, thus earning Victoria-and-Exchange an entry in the record books as the location of the longest platform in Britain (2,194ft).

Externally the two stations presented a contrast. As perhaps might have been expected, the LNWR managed to create an impressive approach, with a

Left: A quiet moment in Manchester Exchange station.

Below: Familiar sights in the LYR's Victoria station were the big Atlantics hauling the heaviest of the expresses. No 708 awaits its turn of duty.   *Ian Allan Library*

broad road leading up to an imposing facade standing well above its surroundings. Victoria, on the other hand, put utility before ostentation; as a contemporary writer tells us, it is 'impossible to gain any idea of its vast interior from a contemplation of the outside; in fact, the outside refuses to be contemplated'.

Over on the other side of the city again, Manchester Central was the 'most commodious and convenient terminus' of the Cheshire Lines, used by Great Central and Midland trains to London as well as their incursions to Liverpool and other parts of Lancashire. Somehow it never quite fulfilled the promise expected by its contemporaries; writing soon after its opening in 1877, F. S. Williams (*The Midland Railway*) believed that the new station, 'being placed in the heart of that great city, adjoining the magnificent Albert Square, the new Town Hall and the Exchange, must become the favourite point of arrival or departure for all parts of the United Kingdom'. Though achieving note for its London and Liverpool expresses, its fame was later eclipsed and, like Exchange, it became a victim of rationalisation.

Above: Having left Exchange, an eastbound LNWR express makes its way through Victoria station for the Stalybridge line. The locomotive is No 1950, *Victorious*, one of the Webb compounds, hauling a train of mixed bogie and six-wheel stock.   *Ian Allan Library*

Below: Road-rail interchange is nothing new: in Bolton the trams had their own station, complete with waiting shelter, in the forecourt of the LNWR Great Moor Street station.   *W. A. Camwell*

Commuter belt

*' Try to spend half an hour on the platform at Victoria.
You will see the earnestness of English industrial and
commercial life — the mill-hand, the artisan, the
warehouseman, the merchant, the banker . . . '*
John Pendleton, *Our Railways*, 1896

Comprehensive though it was, Manchester's railway
network suffered from the lack of any north-south link
across the city centre, a lack which has continued to
the present day. There was no direct connection
between the lines into Victoria and Exchange serving
north Lancashire and Yorkshire, and the lines from the
south into London Road and Central. Moreover, all
these four main stations were themselves situated on
the perimeter of the central area, with none of them as
conveniently placed as it might have been for the
principal business and commercial district. These
factors inevitably affected the role of the railways in
providing local transit, especially after the coming of
the electric tramways and, later, the buses, which
could offer more convenient access.

Local rail traffic was also affected by the nature of
the city's industry and population. Traditionally the
textile industry involved localised employment, with
most workers living within walking distance of the
mills, while the centre of Manchester had become
essentially the hub of commerce rather than
manufacturing. As early as the middle of the 19th
century this transformation had been apparent, as a
description of 1880 reminds us:

'Once a city of mills, Manchester has now become a
city of warehouses. Gradually, as time has progressed,
the manufactories for which it was formerly famous
have been transferred to the surrounding towns and
hamlets, which are now united to the central nucleus
by railways, if not by continuous streets of houses . . . '

Hence the local trains brought in, not so much the
hordes of cheap-fare workmen, but rather the growing
numbers of clerks and shop assistants who served the
commercial heart of the city.

Below: Many of the local LYR stations were modest in
the extreme. This is Bury Knowsley Street in LMS days.
Tramcar and bus provided obvious competition to the
railways on many of the short-distance services.
W. A. Camwell

Suburban traffic can be traced back almost to the earliest days of the railways; by 1845 local services were in operation between Manchester and Stockport, and Manchester and Oldham, while the opening of the railway to Altrincham in 1849 stimulated the development of a 'suburban corridor' between this town and the city. The railways encouraged the suburban spread into the still open areas of the region, where the white-collar workers and the middle classes could make their homes away from the smoke of industry. They also enabled the prosperous businessman to get away from the source of his wealth altogether, by settling on the Fylde Coast or at Buxton, from where he was able to commute daily by fast train. But not least of the achievements of the railways was in the pleasure traffic; they made it possible for the great mass of the people to enjoy a holiday at the seaside or a day in the country at low fares, thus enhancing the quality of life for many whose daily round was confined to the toil of industry.

Despite the competition of electric tramways, residential traffic on the railways was still heavy in the years before 1914; the railways were not only faster than the trams over the longer distances, but they served many areas beyond the extent of the tramways. At Exchange, a substantial residential traffic included busy services connecting with the town of Eccles, a favourite place of residence with many who worked in Manchester and Salford; while in the south the LNWR's expanding commuter traffic obliged it to extend the facilities at London Road by adding a new station, Mayfield. The southern suburbs of Manchester and the district around Stockport were growing to such a extent as residential areas for the city's people that the LNWR ran nearly seventy trains a day for local traffic, carrying about 10,000 passengers daily to and from their homes.

An important addition to the facilities on this side of Manchester was the opening in 1909 of the LNWR's new line between Levenshulme and Wilmslow. Some nine miles in length, it was intended to achieve two purposes: to provide an avoiding loop to relieve the existing overcrowded main line as an alternative to widening this route, and, no less significant, to open up a new area for suburban development. Brought into use for freight on 8 February 1909, it was fully operational for passenger traffic on 1 May following.

Leaving the main line from London Road at Slade

Below: 'Vast throngs of clerical and other workers in Manchester make their homes in the southern suburban districts that are so well served by the "premier" company' (*The Railway Magazine*, 1912). Here an LNWR local hauled by a 4ft 6in Webb 2-4-2 tank passes Heaton Lodge Junction. *Ian Allan Library*

Above right: The Webb 2-4-2 tanks were familiar sights on the LNWR Manchester services; here No 965 stands at Heaton Chapel. *Ian Allan Library*

Right: One for the spotters was a 3-cylinder compound version of the LNWR 2-4-2T, its non-coupled wheels making it a 2-2-2-2T; still with 4ft 6in wheels, it had two high pressure cylinders and one low pressure. No 687 is at Heaton Chapel. *Ian Allan Library*

Lane Junction, the new railway traversed a relatively undeveloped area through Gatley and Styal to rejoin the main line at Wilmslow. Stations were constructed at Mauldeth Road, Didsbury, Gatley, Heald Green and Styal, with a further station at Burnage opened in 1910. Initially the local service comprised about ten trains a day each way, the number still being limited by the accommodation at London Road before the opening of Mayfield, and some trains had to be dealt with at Oxford Road. Stopping trains traversing the new line took 32min to make the journey between Manchester and Wilmslow.

A journey in its first days reveals the nature of the line and the potential which was realised as development took place in the later years. Leaving London Road at Slade Lane, the new line reached its first station about three miles out. Mauldeth Road for Withington was situated in what had long been among the pleasantest suburbs on the southern side of the city, and further residential housing was underway. The next station, Didsbury (later East Didsbury & Parrs Wood), was on the main road from Manchester to Wilmslow; the area was dignified by what were described by a contemporary as 'several large country residences'. Not much more than a mile further south, having crossed the Cheshire Lines, the new railway entered Gatley, which was then depicted as 'a village of no great importance'.

Another mile and a half, through an area containing many market gardens, brought the line into Heald Green station, which was a small structure since, like its neighbour, it also served only a small village. A mile and a half more, and Styal was reached; this served the nearby village and was surrounded by 'many fine country houses', a rustic retreat where Manchester residents could enjoy peace and tranquillity. All the stations were provided with goods facilities, including horse and carriage docks intended to handle the private traffic of their prosperous clientele.

Traversing well wooded countryside, the railway continued to rejoin the main line at Wilmslow, where in consequence a new station had been built. Wilmslow already had a population of some 13,000 and was a popular residential area with a growing com-

Above: The little Webb 2-4-0 tanks produced smart working on the LNWR to Buxton with the morning and evening trains for Manchester businessmen. E. L. Ahrons reported their best run from Buxton to Stockport, over 19 miles, in 32min with seven six-wheelers — good going for a small engine with 4ft 7½in driving wheels. *Ian Allan Library*

Below: Wellknown on the LYR local services were the Barton-Wright 0-4-4 tanks, a design dating from 1877. One of a total of 72, No 112 was withdrawn in 1910. *Ian Allan Library*

muter traffic. Among its attractions were a modern town centre, a golf course and pleasant country walks. Added to this was the improved train service with the coming of the new line, giving fast trains into Manchester in a time of only 20min.

Other residential traffic out of London Road included the service to Buxton, which was becoming a favourite home ground for Manchester businessmen. Smart working was required of the morning and evening business trains in covering the 25 miles through the Peak District where gradients were as steep as 1 in 60.

From Manchester Central, the Cheshire Lines had encouraged development to the south-west, through Trafford Park and on to Urmston, Flixton and Irlam. As early as 1898 increasing traffic had called for the reconstruction of the line between Old Trafford and Chorlton Junction, where the CLC and the Midland lines diverged. Coupled with this was the need to rebuild Chorlton station; as residential property sprang up and suburban passengers increased, the small station had proved quite inadequate, and some of the nearby agricultural land had to be taken over to allow for the extension of the station.

Among other services were those of the Midland Railway, which in 1881 had completed its line via Heaton Mersey and the CLC, thus obtaining access to Central. It operated an out-and-back service from Central to London Road via Stockport, behind 0-4-4 tanks. Another out-and-back route between Central

and London Road was inaugurated in 1892 by the MSL via Levenshulme and Fallowfield; this seems to have got off to a slow start, according to early suburbanites who told stories of a two-mile journey taking six hours and a train being left forgotten in a cutting. Hopes that the line ultimately could have become a complete circle around the city were not to be realised.

Out of Victoria, which handled daily 20,000 season ticket or 'contract' holders, one of the intensive services was that to Oldham, with a total of 46 departures daily. Traversing a heavily built-up area, the line to Oldham and on to Rochdale was a busy one for both passenger and freight traffic. It included the notorious 1 in 27 climb up from Middleton Junction to Werneth, the steepest gradient to carry a regular passenger service; originally cable-assisted, it was by-passed in 1880 by the construction of the line via Hollinwood which had a comparatively easy profile with nothing worse than 1 in 50! The LYR used a powerful class of 0-6-2 tank dating from 1881-82, and for a time these engines had almost a monopoly of the

For many years the mainstay of the Lancashire & Yorkshire local services (as well as almost anything else that came their way) were the 2-4-2 tanks, which numbered 330 in all. As well as working local trains to Oldham, Rochdale and Bury, they were also to be seen on workings to Blackpool and Southport. *Above* is No 337, one of the original batch with short bunker, dating from 1892; *below*, No 297 of 1898 is one of the second type as built with larger bunker. *Ian Allan Library*

LYR's Manchester local services until the arrival of the first of the 2-4-2 tanks which became practically the symbol of the Lancashire & Yorkshire.

In 1890 20 of the 2-4-2 tanks were put to work in the Manchester area, where they were still to be found in the 1920s on Oldham and Rochdale trains of five, six or seven bogie coaches, or pounding up to Werneth with a three-coach shuttle. For a time they were challenged by the short-lived 2-6-2 tanks which had been specially built in 1903-04 for working the severe Bury, Oldham and Stalybridge lines, but these were

soon withdrawn and the 2-4-2 tanks again reigned supreme, until the big Hughes 4-6-4 tanks came along to take some of the heavier workings.

From Oldham, something of a satellite suburban service filtered eastward up into the foothills of the Pennines. The service from Oldfield to Greenfield and on to the branch to Delph had been poor up to the early years of the century, but around 1911 a motor train was introduced and new halts were installed at Grasscroft, and at Moorgate and Dobcross on the branch. This encouraged some new housing development in the area, and by the mid-1920s 36 trains worked each way between Oldham and Greenfield, with 19 on the Delph branch.

An example of the competition the railways had to contend with after the opening of the electric tramways could be seen between Manchester and Middleton, on which route the trams started in 1902. The tram fare for the six miles was $3\frac{1}{2}$d, and although at 40min the journey took longer than the train, the third class return rail fare was 8d, and many people had to look carefuly even at one penny. The trams were more frequent and passed the end of the street, while Middleton station suffered from being the terminus of a short branch from the main line.

The suburban line par excellence was the Manchester South Junction & Altrincham Railway. This had a long history, having been opened on 20 July 1849 from Oxford Road (it was extended through to London Road a few days later) to Altrinc-ham, which was described at the time as 'a particularly clean and neat market town', where 'the chief employment of the labouring classes is agriculture'. In due course Altrincham and the district served by the nine-mile line lost much of its pastoral character and became a popular residential area, the 'South Junction' establishing itself as one of the major suburban railways of the city.

Service on the South Junction was intense; the morning peak saw as many as 14 trains into Manchester in one hour. The standard train in the early years of this century comprised a dozen six-wheelers, hauled by a Great Central tank, either a 2-4-2T or an older 2-4-0T. Punctuality as well as intensity seems to have been notable, earning the line the slogan 'Many Short Journeys and Absolute Regularity' (alternatively 'Many Sharp Jerks and Away', which perhaps reflected the lively running). Sports enthusiasts also came to know the line, since it served the Old Trafford cricket ground where a special station was brought into use on the occasion of important matches; it was claimed that for such events as many as 16 special trains could be loaded and despatched within 45min. Eventually electrification took place in 1931, at which time the normal train service consisted of about 80 trains each way daily, the majority stopping at all stations and taking 25-27min while a few missed out some stations and completed the journey in only 15 to 17min.

A less conventional form of local working was introduced in 1922 between Manchester and Atherton by the LYR in the form of a 'reversible' train, later more widely known as a 'push-and-pull'. A 2-4-2 tank was coupled to an adapted two-car train, with driver's compartment at the outer end from which control was by a compressed air system. One or two similar two-car sets could be added to make up to a six-coach train according to traffic requirements.

Below: No 1450 was one of the massive 2-6-2 tanks of 1903-04, used by the LYR for a time on the heavily graded Manchester local lines to Oldham, Rochdale and Bury. They were fairly soon displaced by the smaller and more serviceable 2-4-2Ts. *Ian Allan Library*

Clubs and wakes

'If Ah was you, Ah'd tak that lass o' thine away on a holiday. Me and y' ma'd only one in us lives, but it were worth it . . . '
        Walter Greenwood, *Love on the Dole*, 1933

Manchester's railways could have presented few greater contrasts than the Club train and the Wakes Week special; between them they stood for the extremes in rail travel, epitomising two distinctive ways of life. One of the institutions of the city's rail services, the Club train was the mode of daily travel for a select class of prosperous merchants and businessmen who worked in Manchester but could afford the time and the money to make their home far away from the industry that created their wealth.

The idea of the Club train seems to have orginated during the 1890s among some of the long-distance commuters from the Fylde Coast. They disliked the idea of sharing their daily journey with the common herd, or of struggling to find a seat during the holiday season when the multitude were seeking their pleasure by the sea at Blackpool. Because they 'wished to be spared the obtrusiveness of the cheap tripper', they were accused of 'priggery, snobbishness and exclusiveness', in the words of a contemporary; nevertheless, they pursued their scheme and accordingly the 'Lytham, St Anne's and Blackpool Travelling Club' was established.

A committee representing first class season ticket holders had been established in 1895 to negotiate with the Lancashire & Yorkshire for the provision of special accommodation for members of the club. The LYR did not take to the idea too enthusiastically at first, but eventually it agreed to provide two 'handsome specially built saloon carriages' in which the members of the club might travel. These carriages were to be attached to a morning train from Blackpool to Manchester, where they would wait until the return journey in the evening. The club had to guarantee a minimum of forty members, who would pay an extra charge for their privileged travel in addition to their first class season ticket. Initially a single saloon was attached to each of two morning trains from Blackpool, while the two together were put on to the 5.10pm from Manchester Victoria.

Furnishings and facilities of the Club coaches were obviously designed to appeal to the tastes of their exclusive occupants. The saloon was provided with easy chairs and tables, there was a special compartment for smokers, and the walls of the saloon were decorated with 'pictures of exceptional artistic merit'. Members generally had their own particular seats which they occupied morning and evening, while strict rules were imposed — windows, for example, were not to be opened. To minister to their needs, the LYR supplied an attendant to travel in each carriage, his duties including 'seeing to the creature comforts of members, and manipulating the ventilation and illuminant'. Refreshments were also made available, again being served by the attendant.

Such was the success of the scheme that soon a third saloon was put on, while other Club Trains were also introduced to cater for residents in Southport, Llandudno and the Lake District. The new Llandudno Club Train introduced by the LNWR in 1907, for example, was described as 'the last word in railway comfort and all that can be desired'. Its interior appears to have reached new heights of opulence, to judge by a contemporary account in *The Railway Magazine*:

Left: How the first class Manchester commuter travelled in Edwardian days: the luxurious interior of one of the 'Club' coaches run between Manchester and Blackpool.

The panelling is of fumed mahogany, bound with green ebony, beading and cross-beading in tulip wood inlay. Black American walnut framing, carved mouldings, and seats of Australian bentwood, together with electric lighting and special lockers for the club members, all combine to make the coaches an ideal club train.

A glance at the typical schedule of one of the club trains gives us an insight into the life style of its fortunate patrons. A morning train left Blackpool Central at 8.10, calling at Lytham at 8.31. Salford, where many alighted for the central business district, was reached at 9.36 and Victoria 9.40. On the return in the evening, the 5.10 from Victoria covered the 50 miles to Blackpool in about 1hr 20min. For the commuter from Windermere the morning train departed at 8.30 and reached Manchester at 10.30, returning also at 5.10 in the evening to arrive back at Windermere at 7.20. From Llandudno the morning departure was at 8.10, with a two-hour journey to Manchester, but with an earlier evening departure at 4.55 and an arrival home at 7.03 after the 88 miles. In all cases these times suggest shorter office hours than those enjoyed by humbler members of the staff.

And the cost of this daily marathon? A typical pre-1914 season ticket rate between Manchester and

Above: After the day's work: a Lancashire & Yorkshire Railway 'Highflier' 4-4-2 pulls out of Manchester with the 5.10pm Blackpool 'Club' train. *Ian Allan Library*

Above right: Unimpressive its exterior may have been, but to many Manchester Victoria station was the gateway to the world of seaside and country.

Right: 'The most vivid impression of a Lancashire crowd is to be obtained on the platform of the Lancashire & Yorkshire company's station', wrote John Pendleton in *Our Railways* (1896). Maybe he had observed scenes such as this at Manchester Victoria as the holiday crowds awaited their trains to Blackpool and other resorts.

Blackpool first class was £31 12s (£31.60) annually, in addition to which of course you had to pay your membership fee if you wanted to travel in the special Club saloons. Club trains continued up to World War 2, by which time the former ornate saloons of the old companies had given way to more standard LMS vehicles, even if some elaboration was applied to uphold their dignified tradition.

For the less affluent, whose everyday life was bounded by Manchester's city streets, the unassuming entrance to Victoria station was the gateway to a

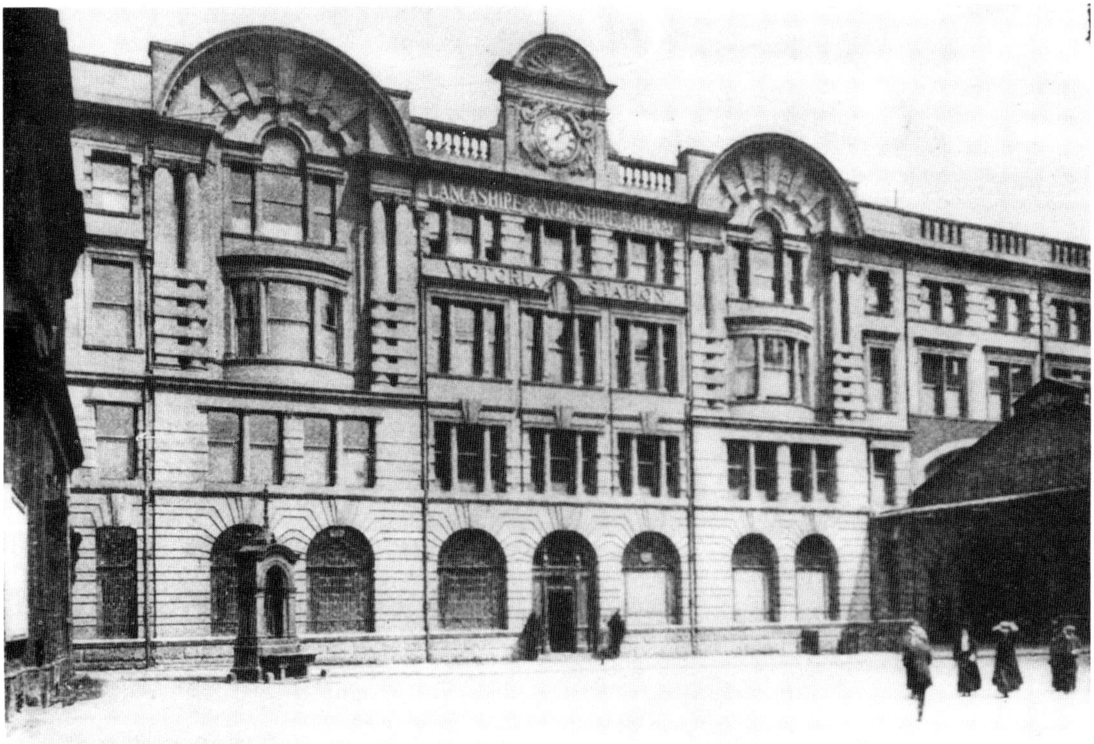
LANCASHIRE & YORKSHIRE RAILWAY
VICTORIA STATION

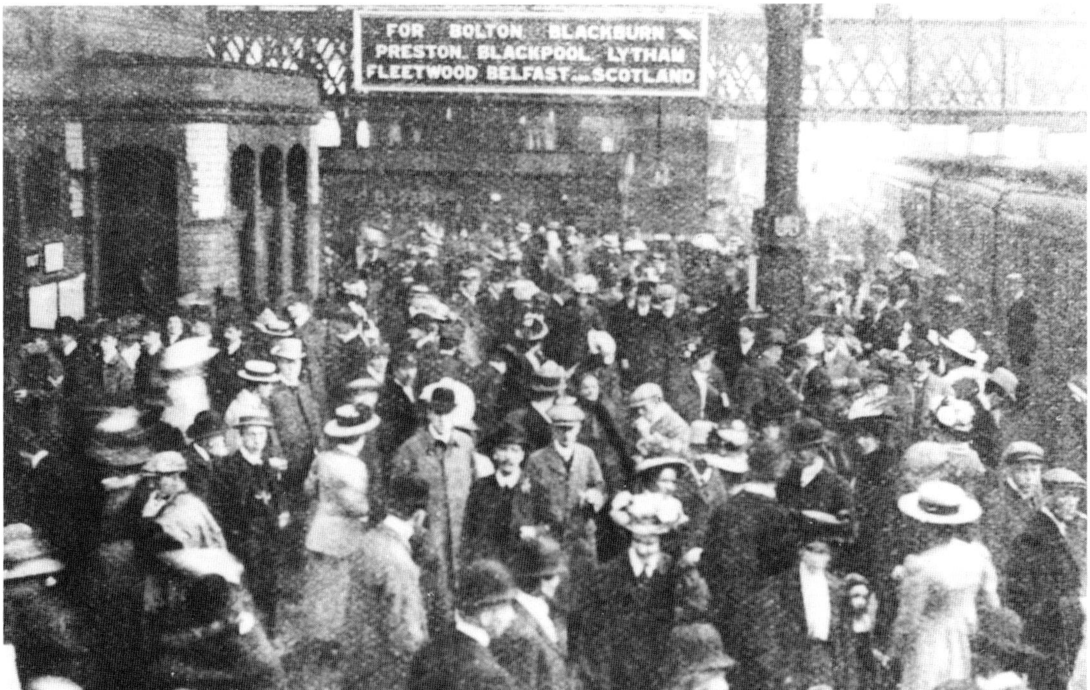
FOR BOLTON. BLACKBURN
PRESTON. BLACKPOOL. LYTHAM
FLEETWOOD BELFAST AND SCOTLAND

world of enchantment. Highlight of their year was 'Wakes Week', when in effect the whole of the industry in a particular town closed down and the workers went off en masse for their annual holiday. The dates of wakes weeks varied from place to place, but together they continued throughout the area from mid-June to about the end of September; workers joined their local 'going away' club in order to save up during the year for the event.

In *Our Railways* (1896) John Pendleton gives us a picture of the 'going away'. 'The operatives work hard and deftly in the mills,' he tells us, 'but they delight to break away from their toil. The mills are closed for a week, and the hands with the pleasant ring of gold in their pockets, and feeling more like cotton lords than doublers and minders, buy fine raiment and much food, and travel'. For the Oldham Wakes Week in August 1892, for example, 'the enormous sum of £80,000 — sufficient to build and fit a cotton mill — was paid out to the operatives from the "going away clubs", and thousands of hands went to Blackpool, Southport, the Isle of Man, and more distant resorts'.

Right: From 1905 the London & North Western Railway's 'Sunny South Special' provided a useful through service from Manchester to Brighton and Eastbourne.

Below: Off to the coast! Leaving the cares of the city behind, a heavy LYR express, hauled by a Hughes 4-6-0, takes water at Walkden troughs. *Ian Allan Library*

For the railways, the Wakes put heavy extra loads on the services, as the workers from each town in turn descended on the trains; far from the luxury of club saloons, even the hardest and severest of the Lancashire and Yorkshire's rolling stock found its way to the seaside.

Premier place among holiday destinations for the people of the Manchester area was of course Blackpool, where Lancashire folk comprised the majority of the 2 million visitors a year. It was not unusual for Manchester alone to send off a dozen crowded trains to Blackpool before noon on a summer Saturday, while more specials departed from other towns such as Bolton, Oldham and Rochdale, so that a procession of trains wound its way to the coast.

If you could afford something different and fancied adventure in that strange land of Southern England, the 'Sunny South Express' made its appearance in 1904 in the shape of through coaches between Manchester and the Sussex resort of Brighton. Such was the success of the new service, that in the following year it blossomed forth into a full scale express, complete with restaurant car, working from both Manchester and Liverpool to Eastbourne as well as Brighton. You could leave Manchester at 10.40am and

Below: For Mancunians, Blackpool was the holiday Mecca, and posters such as these examples from the Edwardian era were a familiar sight.

enjoy a good day's train journey before reaching your holiday destination of Brighton at 4.55 or Eastbourne at 5.45 in the afternoon.

If you just wanted to escape from Manchester for a day, there were plenty of excursions to choose, perhaps the most exciting being those involving a sea voyage, even if this crossed no oceans more expansive that the Irish Sea or the Welsh coastal waters. You could leave Exchange by the 9 o'clock train in the morning, travel to Liverpool nonstop in 40min, then change to an omnibus which took you free of charge down to the quayside for the Isle of Man steamer. This sailed at 10.30, arriving at Douglas at 1.45. Here you had a brief stay of less than two hours on the island before sailing back again for Liverpool, which was reached just before 8 o'clock, to take the train back again to the workaday world of Manchester. Total cost of this combined rail and steamer excursion of more than 200 miles was only 8s 6d (42½p), a rate of travel of more than two miles for a penny.

An alternative way to the Isle of Man was by the LYR route via Fleetwood. On this you left Victoria on the special boat express at 8.55 in the morning, reaching Fleetwood at 10.12. The steamer sailed at 10.30, arriving at Douglas at 1.10, giving you nearly three hours on the island before starting the return journey, which was completed in 4¾hrs. Again the fare was 8s 6d.

Another popular destination for a day out was Llandudno. From Manchester you went to Liverpool, where the splendid steamer *La Marguerite* was waiting at the landing stage for the two-hour voyage along the Welsh coast to Llandudno. You stayed here about four hours, the steamer being due back at Liverpool at 7.30, whence you took the train home again to Manchester. The fare for this day's travel was 8s (40p). Again combining sea and scenery was the excursion to Windermere, also leaving Manchester at 8.55 for Fleetwood but this time embarking on the Furness Railway's *Philomel* or *Lady Evelyn* for the hour's voyage to Barrow. Here you took the train to Lake Side to board the company's steam yacht for the serene joys of Lake Windermere as far as Bowness. A short walk to Windermere station enabled you to get a train back to Manchester in about three hours. The fare for this 170 miles of rail, sea and lake was just 5s 3d (26p).

Less ambitious itineraries were provided for a half-day's outing, one example introduced by the LYR in 1909 being known as a 'picnic train'. Behind this was the realisation that with the growth of the built-up area it was neccessary to go further afield in order to find the real countryside. So on Saturday, at 1.20pm, the 'picnic train' departed from Manchester bound for Whalley and Clitheroe, calling on the way to pick up at Bolton, Darwen and Blackburn. The return train left Clitheroe at 8.19pm and Whalley at 8.26, 'giving passengers about six hours stay in this picturesque neighbourhood', as the LYR informed us. Nearer home, Manchester's Belle Vue gardens were a centre of attraction. Evening excursions pulled into Ashburys station to bring thousands to enjoy the delights of the gardens, including a menagerie, dancing and firework displays.

Right: The LYR advertises its 'Picnic Train' for the benefit of day trippers from Manchester.

3
Tramcars in their glory

Municipal enterprise

'Today Manchester has a well-equipped and capably-managed electrical tramway system of which any Corporation might be proud . . . In this great city the people have been endowed with a mobility for purposes of both business and pleasure which is little less than a revelation.'

Tramway and Railway World, 1906

If one single feature stands out as marking the social significance of urban transit facilities, it is surely the extension of those facilities to meet the needs of the great mass of the townspeople. The early coach and the omnibus were the vehicles of the bourgeoisie; they served the comparatively select few who could afford to make their homes in leafy suburbs away from the smoke of industry. The tramway was the great proletarian mover; it extended the privilege of easy transit to the large numbers of the ordinary people. And, as far as the Greater Manchester region was concerned, the electric tramways were essentially an element of municipal service, aiming to bring the benefits of cheap and convenient transport within the reach of as many people as possible.

With the growth of the urban population during the 19th century, there was at the same time a growth in urban identity; the older forms of local government based on rural England had to be displaced by new forms more suited to the new conditions. Manchester, which Defoe had described in the 18th century as 'the greatest mere village in England' on account of its rudimentary local government, became a borough in 1838 and attained the status of a city in 1853. Other growing towns also achieved a new dignity: Oldham was incorporated as a borough in 1849, Rochdale in 1856 and Bury in 1876.

An important step forward came with the Local Government Act of 1888. This not only set up county councils to replace the older administrative machinery, but also gave nearly all towns with a population of more than 50,000 the status of county borough and with it a large measure of autonomy in running their own affairs. A further Act in 1894 served to establish more new local government units, the boroughs and urban districts. Hence by the end of the century, the towns — including the Lancashire industrial towns

which had grown so rapidly — were not only becoming more formally organised, but were taking on a new dignity and becoming aware of their powers and their influence.

Part of this process was an increasing interest in municipal trading. Many local authorities engaged in the production of gas for domestic purposes, in the provision of water supplies, and in the ownership of markets and other amenities as part of their service to their ratepayers. By the last years of the 19th century, electricity became another field of municipal action; often allied with the supply of electricity to domestic and industrial consumers, one particular application of electricity appeared to be the coming thing, namely the electric tramway.

Many towns, of course, already had tramways in their streets; the Manchester Carriage & Tramways Company served both Manchester and the surrounding towns and suburbs. But although the local authorities might own the tracks within their respective areas, they were not the operators of the tramways. Under the terms of the Tramways Act of 1870 local authorities were enabled to construct tramways, but they were expected to leave the working of them to private enterprise, in this case the Manchester company. But now that local authorities were duly reformed and were already engaging in all kinds of trading, why should they not further extend their interests into tramway operation? Surely the supply of local transport was as legitimate a matter of civic concern as the supply of gas or water?

As it happened, this upsurge in municipal pride coincided with a time when the means of achieving this ambition was to hand. The Tramways Act had also made provision for compulsory purchase of tramway undertakings by local authorities, generally after a period of 21 years or at intervals thereafter, and since many systems had been constructed during the 1870s and 1880s this time was now falling due.

Another happy coincidence was that at this period the application of electric operation to tramways had become a practical proposition. It was clear that the future lay with electricity; while the horse-drawn cars had served well, they were now outclassed by reason of the additional speed, facility and economy made possible with electric traction. But the introduction of

Left: 'No provincial town in Britain can boast of a more sumptuous set of public buildings or finer streets than this emporium of the cotton trade' (*Our Own Country*, 1880). Manchester Royal Exchange by the early years of the twentieth century was joined by another symbol of civic pride — the electric tramway — and the photographer felt obliged to move with the times by painting out the horses from the tram and drawing in overhead wires.

Below: The new electric tramways transformed the city streets as they brought fast and frequent services; by 1907 Manchester Corporation had more than 500 cars — here a few of them illustrate the intensity of service along Piccadilly. On the left the old Infirmary still occupies its commanding site. *R. Brook*

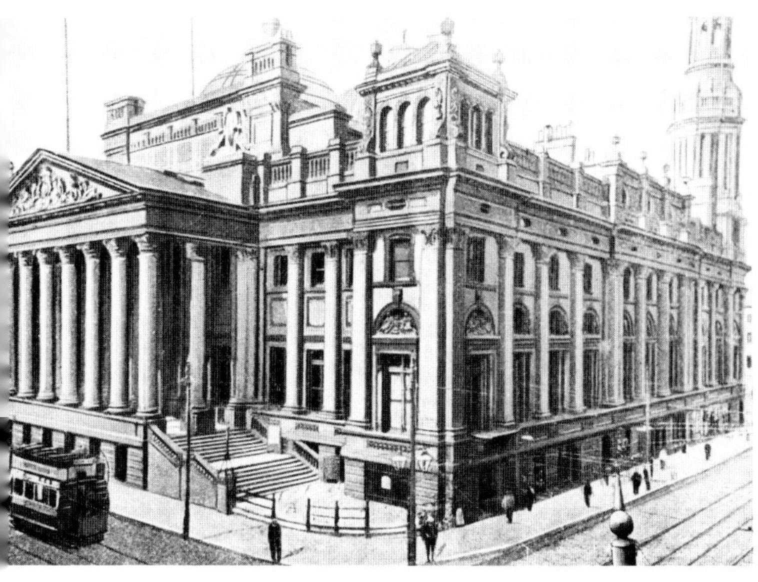

electric traction involved the investment of large sums of money; and the companies, with their leases due to expire soon and with the threat of compulsory purchase hanging over them, were not inclined to invest sums of money on which they were not likely to survive long enough to see a worthwhile return. So the tramways continued to be powered by horses, to become less attractive as equipment got older and more decrepit, and so to add further weight to the argument for municipal acquisition. Everything conspired towards municipalisation and electrification, so that the years around the turn of the century saw a burgeoning of municipal electric tramways, to inaugurate a new era in urban transport and civic enterprise.

In Greater Manchester this process marked the end of the 'empire' of the Manchester Carriage & Tramways Company and the displacement of its services by new municipally-operated electric tramcars, which also penetrated to areas where trams had never been seen before. In Manchester itself, the corporation took over the company's lines, electrified them and began operating its own system on 6 June 1901. The same year saw municipal operations started

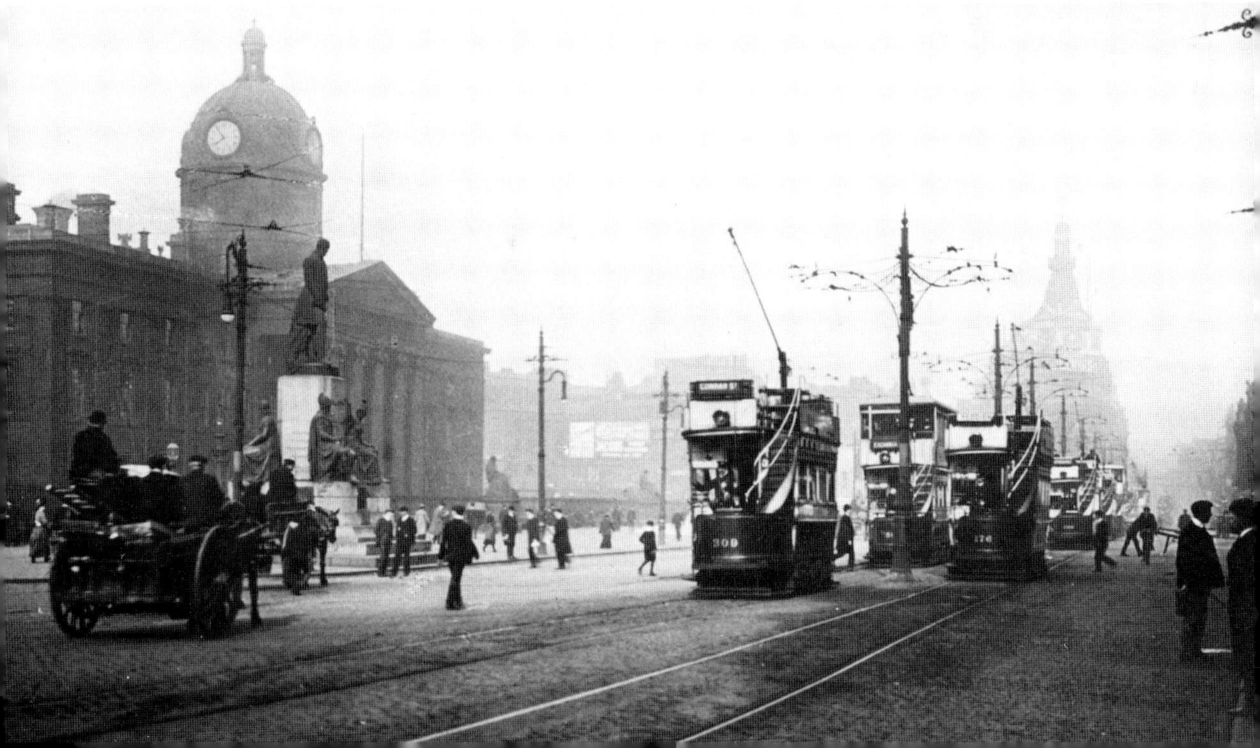

Above: The opening of a new electric tramway was an occasion for civic rejoicing; such scenes as this were common in the years of the tramway boom, although the great days of expansion were almost over when Bolton Corporation opened its Darcy Lever route in 1910 with specially built single-deckers. *R. Brook*

Centre right: By contrast there is almost a Wild West air about this extension of the Rochdale tramways, as civic officials inspect a new route climbing into the Pennines. The elaborate bracket standard is noteworthy, as is the old car body doing duty as a waiting shelter on this exposed section of line. *R. Brook*

Below right: The quintessential Lancashire 'tramscape': a tangle of tracks and glittering setts as cars cross and recross. The junction of Regent Road and Oldfield Road in Salford. *W. A. Camwell*

in Salford on 4 October. Oldham Corporation had already inaugurated its own electric tramways on 15 December 1900, while Rochdale came later, on 22 May 1902.

First in the field had been Bolton, where the corporation obtained powers, under the Bolton Tramways & Improvement Act of 1897, for the working of the town's tramways itself. The first trams in Bolton had been proposed as early as 1877, when the corporation in conjunction with a company which was already providing omnibus services drew up a plan for the construction of a system. Under the Bolton & Suburban Tramways Act 1878, promoted by Bolton Corporation together with the local authorities of the districts of Astley Bridge, Farnworth and Kearsley, construction was authorised, the first lines opening in 1879. Though the tracks were owned by the local authorities, they were leased to the company which carried out the actual operation. Following the 1897 Act, Bolton Corporation arranged with the company for the transfer of its interests to the corporation and to the other local authorities from which they were leased, and then on 9 December 1899 the first of the corporation's electric cars began service.

Once under way, the new municipal electric tramway systems expanded rapidly, with new and extended routes, growing fleets of cars, and with increasing numbers of passengers. In Manchester, for example, the corporation's fleet of cars had grown to more than 500 by 1907, operating over more than 90 miles of routes; the number of passengers carried increased to over 140 million from only 24 million in 1902.

Within a few years a network of electric tramways had been constructed across the Greater Manchester area, extending from the foothills of the Pennines to the mouth of the Mersey, from the North Lancashire hills to the plains of Cheshire. From Mossley, through Ashton, Manchester and Salford, to Wigan and Atherton (where the tracks continued to St Helens and Liverpool) was some 25 miles as the crow flies, while from Bacup, through Rochdale, Manchester and Stockport to Hazel Grove was another 25 miles. Routes varied in character from busy main streets with a constant procession of big double-deckers, to semi-rural roads where one car every half hour sufficed.

By 1911 the municipal tramways of the Greater Manchester area in the hands of ten operators served a population of nearly $2\frac{1}{2}$ million people. About a thousand cars were in daily service over more than 300 miles of routes, carrying well over 300 million passengers a year. Several of the municipalities undertook the operation of lines owned by non-operating local authorities, while joint working agreements permitted the running of through services between towns.

Top: In the type of industrial landscape that inspired artist L. S. Lowry, Oldham Corporation No 19 (a 1924 English Electric car) stands at Shaw, Wren's Nest, terminus. *W. A. Camwell*

Above: The new electric tramways served to link hitherto outlying communities to the nearby towns; this is the Healey terminus of the Rochdale system before the line was extended even further to reach Bacup. *R. Brook*

Left: Most of the SHMD Board routes consisted of single track along narrow streets, such as Manchester Road, Mossley.   *R. Brook*

Below left: Almost a country village atmosphere about the tram terminus at Haughton Green when the Manchester electric cars first arrived to connect it with the big city. Open-top car No 137, one of the large number of Manchester's Brush-built four-wheelers of 1901-3, prepares to depart for Denton.   *R. Brook*

Bottom: Typical of the early generation of electric tramcars was this Hurst Nelson four-wheeler of 1905, No 47 in the fleet of the SHMD Board. It is prominently lettered 'SHMD Joint Tramways'. By the time it was photographed here outside the Tame Street depot, in 1937, it was the last open-topper.   *W. A. Camwell*

Right: 'Bolton's repair workshops were completed in 1913; they are well laid out on the most up to date lines. All necessary repairs, including rebuilding and painting, are carried out here' (*Tramway and Railway World*). Extensive rebuilding was often undertaken and the tramcar generally had a long life.   *R. Brook*

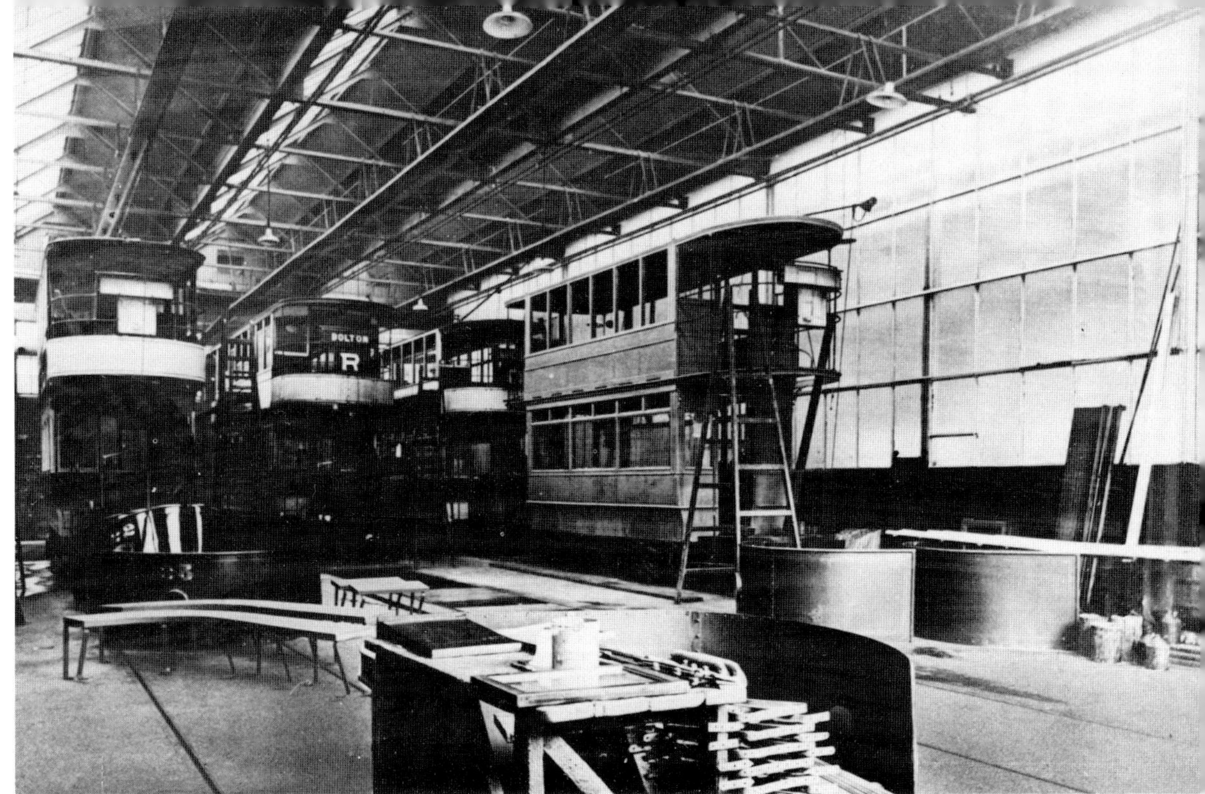

The average fare per mile amounted to 0.7d, varying from only 0.4d on the large-scale Manchester undertaking to 0.9d in Rochdale where some of the routes were more sparsely trafficked. The distance you could travel for a 1d fare averaged 1.35 miles, again with variations from only 0.8 mile in Rochdale again to as far as 2.3 miles in Manchester. The average fare paid per passenger was 1.2d, varying from 0.9d on the SHMD to 1.5d in Rochdale, so that the average traveller rode the tram for a distance of just over 1.5 miles. (For the present-day equivalent of these figures, 2.4d equals 1p, so that the average fare was equal to $\frac{1}{2}$p).

Not every individual municipality went its own way; four of them decided to get together and form one of those rare organisations in local government, a joint board. The object was to provide a service which required to extend over an area larger than that of one local authority if it was to be an economic proposition, and which called for an expenditure held to be beyond the means of one authority by itself. Hence the Stalybridge, Hyde, Mossley & Dukinfield Tramways & Electricity Board (referred to as 'SHMD' for short, since it must have had one of the longest titles in the business) was set up in 1901 under an Act of Parliament enabling the four municipalities named in its title to establish a jointly owned and managed organisation to look after their tramways and their electricity concerns. Each of the four corporations sent six

representatives to a board of management which was placed in charge of the undertakings. Any surplus made on the tramways, after allowing for the necessary charges, was to be distributed in equal shares to the four partners, while by the same token any loss had to be borne equally. Losses on the tramways could be offset by profits on the electricity undertaking, and vice versa.

All four towns involved were of modest size and resources, and the installation by each of its own tramways would probably have produced systems too small to be economically viable, whereas taken all together the affair was of reasonable size, with a fleet that at its maximum totalled about 40 cars.

Establishment of the board was in large part a reaction against local proposals by the British Electric Traction Company, which owned the nearby Oldham, Ashton & Hyde Tramways Company, to extend into the areas of the local authorities. They in turn, in the full flight of municipal integrity, decided to forestall this intruder and do the job themselves. The first lines of the new board were opened on 21 May 1904, and routes were constructed to connect the four towns and provide a through service into next-door Ashton.

Most of the board's routes consisted of single track which threaded its way through the narrow streets of the Tame Valley and tended to peter out as it neared the breezy heights of the Pennines. It was not the most intensely trafficked system and not the most profitable, but it served a useful purpose in demonstrating how separate local authorities could cooperate to provide a public service for the benefit of their citizens, and it survived to be incorporated into the PTE.

Municipal tramways were not seen purely as commercial undertakings, and a share of the profits they made was put back into the town's treasury. During their heyday the tramways were contributing substantial sums towards the relief of rates. In the case of Manchester, the amount paid over in 1906 was £50,000, the equivalent of a 3½d rate, and this rose to £75,000 in 1911, to £85,000 in 1912, and to £100,000 in 1913, when it was equal to a 6d (2½p) rate. Nor was Manchester alone in this; in one year, 1911, for example, municipal trams in Salford contributed £18,750 to the relief of rates in that city, while in Bolton the amount was almost £8,000 and in Bury nearly £1,700. While the concept of an integrated municipal economy was doubtless sound, it may be that retention of such sums within the transport undertakings themselves would have helped to ensure their longer-term future. As it is, when we are called upon in the present day to put money into transport undertak-

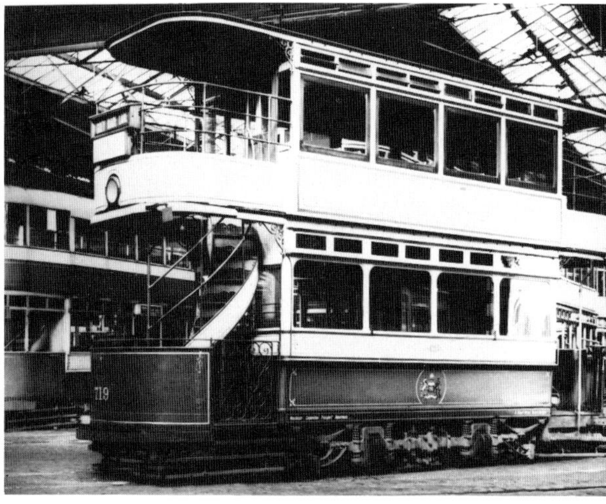

'The Manchester cars are fine examples of elegance and solidity combined, and fitted with all the latest improvements for the comfort of travellers' (A. H. Beavan, *Tube, Train, Tram and Car*, 1903). Both four-wheelers and bogie cars were used, but the larger vehicles soon became standardised for the most heavily-trafficked routes. Four-wheeler No 719 *right* was one of 30 constructed by the MCTD in 1912 on Brill 21E trucks; *below*, bogie car No 680 dated from 1909 and was also built by the Department, but mounted on Brill 22E bogies. *W. A. Camwell*

ings in the form of subsidy, we should remember the amounts that were taken out in the past.

In addition to the municipal operators, strategic positions were occupied by three companies, two of which were members of the British Electric Traction group. The Oldham, Ashton & Hyde company's main route between Hyde, Ashton and Hathershaw was part of a proposed system which it intended to build but which did not materialise under company ownership. The company continued in existence until 1921 when its operations were taken over by the municipalities of Ashton, Manchester and the SHMD, enabling through services to be integrated with these three authorities. The other BET company, Middleton Electric Traction, worked in the town of Middleton, and it too was eventually municipalised.

Biggest of the companies was the South Lancashire Tramways, one of the great 'might have beens' of

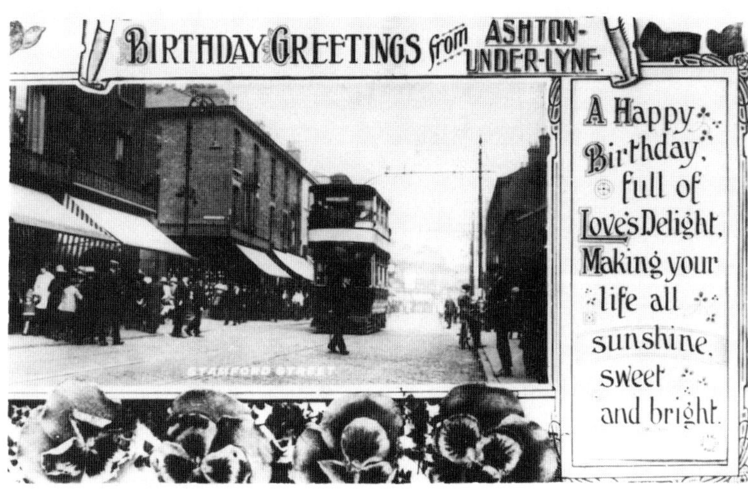

Left: You could even have trams among the flowers on your birthday card: here you got a view of Stamford Street with your 'Birthday Greetings from Ashton-under-Lyne'.   R. Brook

Below: From the cloud of smoke it looks as though the tram is on fire, but it's only one of those new-fangled horseless carriages passing by! South Lancashire Tramways No 8 stands in Market Street, Leigh, preparing to depart for Bolton in the early days of this extensive interurban system.

tramway history. Situated so as to form a crucial last piece in the jigsaw puzzle of the region's tracks, the SLT was the key to the connection between the Manchester area and Merseyside. Its basic role was fulfilled in 1906 when lines were laid in to make possible through services between Manchester and Liverpool, but any dreams this may have inspired that the SLT could have become an interurban empire on the American pattern, with fast electric cars winging their way between Piccadilly and Pier Head, were destined to be disappointed. Still, you could make the journey all the way by tram from Manchester to Liverpool, via Salford and then the SLT's tracks through Worsley, Swinton, Atherton, Ashton-in-Makerfield, and St Helens, to Liverpool, but it was not for the impatient, as *Tramway and Railway World* made clear at the time: 'The journey involves walking about 50 yards, five changes, and the use of six cars. The distance is $39\frac{3}{4}$ miles, the time occupied is five hours, and the fare is 1s 11d'. [Just under 10p]

By contrast, you could make the journey by fast train in 40min, while if your predilection was for cargo steamer by night on the Ship Canal you could have spent eight hours over it.

More than 75 miles of route had been envisaged by the SLT, but in the event only about 30 miles were actually built, the first of them in 1902 when a service started between Lowton, Leigh, Atherton and Four Lane Ends, where the tracks met those of Bolton Corporation. Although most of the proposals never reached fruition, thoughts of electric interurban communication lingered on into the 1920s, when the plan for a grand new highway between Manchester and Liverpool brought suggestions for a reserved track tramway to provide a limited stop express service between the two cities along what was to become the East Lancashire Road.

Though such a service never materialised, through working between one town and another became an essential feature of Greater Manchester's electric tramway network. In 1902 Manchester cars were running into Stockport, while in the next year a through service was started between Stockport and Hyde. In 1906, Rochdale and Oldham were linked, while in 1907 through operation commenced between Manchester and Oldham and Manchester and Ashton, as well as between Bolton and Bury. In 1909 Bury and Rochdale were joined, and the South Lancashire company was running its cars into Bolton. Such was the extent of inter-operation that eventually Manchester, for example, was working 14 joint tram services with six other municipal operators — Ashton, Oldham, Rochdale, Salford, Stockport and the SHMD Board.

Ceremonies at the start of the Manchester-Oldham through service in 1907 demonstrated the importance attached to such arrangements. The formal opening of the service between Piccadilly and Waterhead in Oldham, a distance of nearly nine miles, took place on 21 January with a procession of five decorated cars and a ceremony at the municipal boundary where the Lord Mayor of Manchester cut a tape across the road amid toasts to 'the success of the Oldham and Manchester tramway undertakings and the through service of cars'. Public service started the following day, with a 10min frequency, at a through fare of 6d ($2\frac{1}{2}$p).

Under the terms of the agreement between

Manchester and Oldham, each of the partners secured running powers over the other's tracks, handing over the gross earnings it received as a result of the exercise of these powers. Each provided a proportion of the cars in proportion to its total route mileage, all cars to be as nearly as possible of equal seating capacity. Any excess mileage run by either partner would be paid for on an assessment made in relation to working expenses.

In addition to such through-running agreements, there was another means by which the potential fragmentation of local ownership was averted. Some

Below left: Gateway to the promised land: Moses Gate would have been an important junction on the South Lancashire Tramways if all plans had reached fruition. Here in 1938 Bolton Corporation cars still work through to Farnworth (left) and Walkden (right) but the Bolton-Manchester through service is left to the buses. *W. A. Camwell*

Bolton's interurban: Horwich was little more than a village when the Lancashire & Yorkshire Railway established its locomotive works there in the 1880s, but was already a fair-sized town when the electric tramway from Bolton was opened in 1900.
Right: No 116 (an English Electric bogie car of 1921) pauses at Lostock, the wide Chorley New Road in the distance providing a good racing ground across country.
Below: The route was served by a separate depot at Horwich (lettered 'Bolton Corporation Car Shed'). No 104 (a rebuilt single decker) passes, while Nos 139 and 150 stand in the depot entrance. *W. A. Camwell*

municipalities owned the tracks within their boundaries but, instead of running their own cars, they let the lines out to others to run over. Thus, for example, Manchester Corporation reached agreement to provide services in the areas of the non-operating local authorities of Audenshaw, Denton, Droylsden, Failsworth, Heywood, Middleton, Prestwich, Sale, Stretford and Altrincham. Salford Corporation provided services in Eccles, Swinton, Pendlebury, Prestwich and Whitefield.

Such arrangements were obviously beneficial in improving communication and in helping towards welding the individual undertakings into some kind of

Joint tramway working between Manchester and Oldham started in 1907 and continued until 1946. These two views, taken in 1938, depict the two partners at the extremities of the nine-mile route: *Below:* Oldham Corporation No 11 (an English Electric balcony car of 1921) turns from Piccadilly into Oldham Street to return to its home town. *Right:* Manchester Corporation Pullman car No 287 stands at the Waterhead terminus in Oldham in sight of the Pennines. *Both: W. A. Camwell*

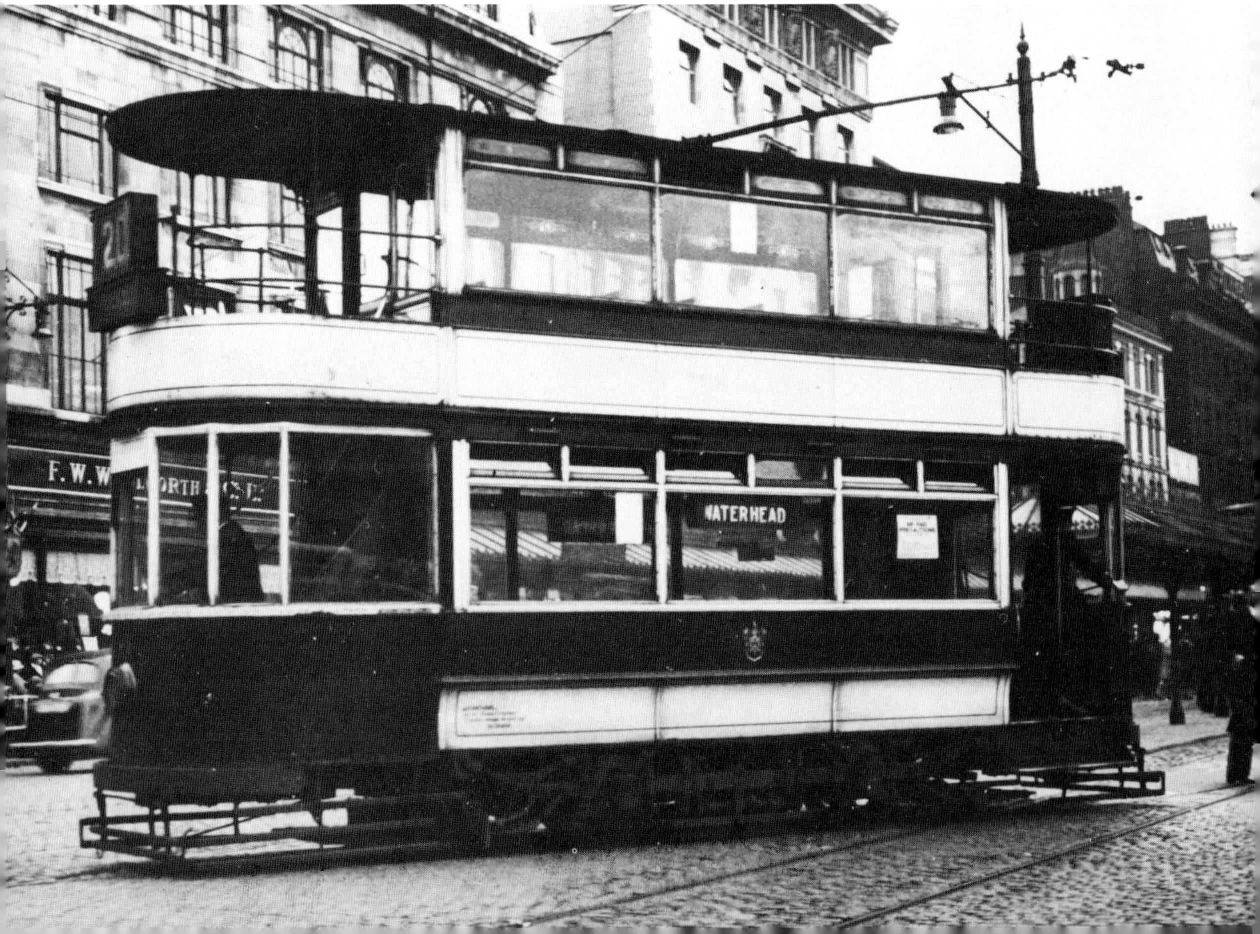

Out-of-town destinations served by Manchester's cars included Ashton and Stockport. *Above*: A Manchester bogie car shares the Hazel Grove terminus with a Stockport four-wheeler; Manchester cars did not work through to this point until 1924. *R. Brook. Right:* Manchester No 229 outside the Town Hall at Ashton-under-Lyne in 1938; another long-lived joint operation, the Manchester-Ashton through service started in 1907. *W. A. Camwell*

coordinated whole. But while many of the agreements dated from the golden age of the tramways when their influence could be most effective, others were so long delayed that by the time they came into existence the motorbus was already demonstrating that it was the most suitable mode for this type of task. A Rochdale-Ashton tram service did not start until 1921, while a through Rochdale-Manchester operation was not in being until 1925 when the formerly independent Middleton system had been municipalised and integrated with adjoining Corporation routes. And by the time the tracks of Salford Corporation and the SLT were connected at Pendlebury in 1928, to make possible a through service between Salford and Bolton, a frequent bus service had already been established, involving not only municipal operators but also companies like Ribble and independents like Tognarelli. Future coordination lay with the motorbus.

The Tram in the community

An insight into the role which the municipal tramways played in the urban environment and the effects which they had on the distribution of population was given by Manchester's tramways manager, J. M. McElroy, in an interview with *Tramway and Railway World* in 1906. In this, McElroy expressed his views on the effects of the new facilities:

'Cheap and rapid transit under commodious conditions tends to spread the population, even in a city like Manchester, where the population, for natural reasons, is exceptionally dense. At the same time, there is a pronounced tendency on the part of a large portion of the working classes to live as near to their work as possible. That, I believe, is an inherent tendency which you cannot alter, but which travelling facilities affect without doubt.'

Answering the objection that the introduction of tramways to the streets resulted in the depreciation of property, he believed that in some instances the value of large residential property along the main routes had been slightly reduced, but that in general improved transport facilities tended to lead to an appreciation in the value of property.

McElroy's opinion (and later events were to prove him correct) was that they were only at the start of a period of change resulting from the fact that the electric tramways had 'revolutionised the whole means of transit. The habits and social customs of the people are being affected ... There is a general tendency all round the city towards growth and development, and I think it safe to say that housing accommodation is increasing'.

The corporation's policy with regard to its

Left: The character of central Manchester in the electric tramway era is epitomised here: the hurrying figures, bent on business; the solid-built Royal Hotel and beyond it the tower of Lewis's; the line of bustling shops; horse-drawn wagons engaged in the city's trade; and through it all sails the new electric tramcar, its poles and wires becoming a familiar part of the street scene. *R. Brook*

Above: 'West of us, well beyond the tramlines, lay the middle classes, bay-windowed and begardened. We knew them not'. (Robert Roberts, *The Classic Slum*). Along Salford's tree-lined middle-class Eccles Old Road, No 33 (one of the Corporation's original Milnes cars of 1901-2) is city-bound. *R. Brook*

Right: Leafy suburbs for Manchester's prosperous middle classes; only a twopenny tram ride from town at Plymouth Grove along the Stockport Road, an enclosed bogie car makes a journey on service 35A. *R. Brook*

tramways was firmly based on two principles. The first was that 'the people on whose credit the capital is raised should have the benefit of low fares'; and that meant of course the ratepayers, for whom a low-fares policy was thus established almost from the beginning. The second principle was that the tramway system 'should be maintained at the point of greatest efficiency, and that every possible precaution, both financial and otherwise, should be taken in the future interests of the systems'. This again meant a sound policy on ensuring the maintenance of valuable assets.

The low fares policy and the role of the tramways are both illustrated in figures relating to fares paid and distance travelled by passengers.

Figures of the percentages of the total passengers carried at different fares clearly illustrate the extent to which the tramways were essentially a short distance mode of transport. About 70% of the total number of passengers were carried at 1d fares, while no less than 95% of total passengers were carried at fares of not more than 2d (less than 1p).

In the light of such figures, it was no wonder that McElroy was able to assert that the local railways must have felt the competition of the tramways within a radius of three or four miles from the city; beyond that, however, 'I do not think we compete seriously'. Linking these fares with the distances they covered, we are able to see the sphere of influence opened up by the tramways.

Manchester Tramways: percentages of passengers carried at various fares 1907

Fare	Percentage of total number of passengers
$\frac{1}{2}$d	6.8
1d	69.2
1$\frac{1}{2}$d	11.9
2d	7.1
2$\frac{1}{2}$d	2.1
3d	1.6
3$\frac{1}{2}$d	0.8
4d	0.4
4$\frac{1}{2}$d	0.1
	100.0

Manchester Tramways: average distance for each fare, 1907

Fare	Average distance
$\frac{1}{2}$d	1,431yd
1d	2 miles 206yd
1$\frac{1}{2}$d	2 miles 1,166yd
2d	3 miles 657yd
2$\frac{1}{2}$d	4 miles 308yd
3d	4 miles 1,465yd
3$\frac{1}{2}$d	5 miles 1,079yd
4d	6 miles 600yd
4$\frac{1}{2}$d	7 miles 262yd

The average fare amounted to just over $\frac{1}{2}$d a mile, with the penny fare taking you more than two miles, while the 2d fare was valid for journeys of over three miles. This obviously brought a substantial area within the range of these fares, including the inner suburbs where the bulk of the traffic was concentrated, since these were the most densely populated parts of the city.

Although further extensions were made to the system, notably into the southern suburbs which were still in the course of development, the basic network had already been established by around 1907. It included the lengthy lines into such growing suburbs as Stretford and the route to Altrincham, as well as to neighbouring towns such as Oldham, Ashton and Stockport, although clearly the through traffic on the lengthier routes was still limited.

In his book *Tramways and Trolleys*, John P. McKay correlates the network with the time taken to reach the different areas of the city and the surrounding districts. He shows that the two-mile ring from the centre of the city (the realm of the penny fare) was all within a 20min journey (including the time taken in walking to the car), while in many instances along the principal radial routes the 20min journey time extended to the three-mile radius (the zone of the 2d fare), the rest of this being within the 30min time zone. Thus the trams not only brought a new era of cheap, fast and convenient transport over the shorter distance in the most heavily populated districts of the city; they also extended the influence of local mass transport far beyond the previous bounds.

A glance at a few individual fares as they stood at this time indicates what your journey cost to some of the extremities of the network. In each case the fare is from the centre of Manchester: 2d Belle Vue, Heaton Park, Fallowfield; 3d Hollinwood, Stretford; 4d Ashton, Stockport.

To put such fares into perspective, it is instructive to recall the level of wages at the time, and the example of

Left: The coming of the tramways encouraged an 'infilling' along the main routes; 'bay-windowed and begardened' housing at Fairfield on Ashton Old Road as Ashton Corporation No 34 (a 1921-vintage English Electric car) pauses for the photographer before continuing its journey into Manchester. *W. A. Camwell*

Below: High-density suburban housing maintained a concentration of traffic along the tram routes; Bolton's Tonge Moor terminus, with a glimpse of the open country beyond. *W. A. Camwell*

Cheap and convenient transport made city shopping and popular entertainment readily accessible to the masses.
Above left: Salford and Manchester trams bring the shoppers to Deansgate.
Left: Manchester trams pass the Hippodrome Theatre in Oxford Road.

Above: 'Manchester contains at its heart a rather extended commercial district, consisting almost wholly of offices and warehouses . . . The district is cut through by certain main thoroughfares upon which the vast traffic concentrates, and in which the ground level is lined with brilliant shops'. Engels' description of 1844 held good for long after. The view from Victoria Bridge some 60 years later shows Manchester top-covered trams in Victoria Street and an open-top Salford car coming from Deansgate. *R. Brook*

the tramwaymen themselves may serve as an illustration. When you took up your appointment as a motorman, your starting pay was 6.22d per hour, rising each year until after four years you were earning 7.5d per hour (about 3p). On the basis of a 54hr week this gave you a weekly pay packet of about £1 14s (£1.70). You had the opportunity of working overtime, of course; you were paid time and a quarter for all time worked over nine hours a day, and time and a half for time worked after 11 hours. For Sundays, you got an extra $\frac{1}{2}$d an hour on all these rates. Such rates of pay were not among the lowest to be obtained, but they are sufficient indication that a daily journey to work involving a fare of 2d or 3d each way could represent an appreciable slice of the personal budget. They are also a reminder of the extent to which a cheap and intensive service was dependent on an abundant supply of low-paid labour.

By 1914 the heavily built-up area had considerably expanded from the former two- or three-mile radius, to extend some four miles or more in all directions from the city, following the major tram routes along the main roads. And on some of these, the built-up area coalesced with that of adjoining towns such as Ashton, Oldham and Stockport, while the former open spaces between the towns were being taken up both with a form of ribbon development along the tramways, and by an infilling of intermediate areas. Taking his time zones again, McKay points out that not only were these neighbouring towns within the 40-50min journey time of central Manchester, but in addition large new areas within a 30-40min time radius were opened up for suburban housing.

McKay further suggests that, whereas in many cities the tramway followed urban development, in the Manchester area the interurban routes when they were constructed ran through areas between the towns which were still not fully built-up; they were laid in

Above: For a penny a schoolchild could travel the whole length of a Bolton tram route, to reach for example the Montserrat terminus where the Chorley Old Road led on to the moors beyond the last houses of the suburbs. *W. A. Camwell*

advance of development. In Manchester, he says, 'tramways were not simply following suburban development, but they were leading that development by extending their services in advance of existing demand'. Although, as we have seen, ribbon development was nothing new (the main road between Manchester and Oldham was practically continuously lined with buildings before the end of the 19th century) the electric tramways did much to make new areas available for housing, and thus helped to relieve the pressure of high population density by encouraging decentralisation.

At the same time as they helped towards the dispersal of population into the suburbs, the tramways also served to concentrate traffic upon the central area. Business and commercial activity was focused within a fairly small central district — one of the basic causes of the problem of congestion which was to occupy the tramways department and other authorities over the years. In Manchester, as McKay points out, 'great and unmistakable concentration was evidenced by both the absence of residential population in the central business districts and by the very pronounced rush hour surges of traffic inward and outward on lines serving the centre'.

This emphasised the fact that the central area of the city was becoming less and less devoted to manufacturing and instead was becoming more concerned with commerce; central streets were lined with offices and shops, counting houses and warehouses, all of which called for increasing numbers of white-collar workers who commuted from the suburbs each day. As Engels found as early as the 1840s, 'nearly the whole district is abandoned by dwellers, and is lonely and deserted at night; only watchmen and policemen traverse its narrow lanes'.

But the tramways also served to bring back life to the central areas beyond the normal business hours. They enabled the ordinary people to travel for purposes of shopping and entertainment. Big-city amenities such as theatres and department stores were brought within easy reach, and flourished accordingly; indeed, local shopkeepers complained that the trams took away their customers who preferred the wider range of goods they could obtain in the big central stores.

The new electric cars also made it easier to get out of the crowded towns for a brief spell in the open country, a feature which helped to widen the horizons of the younger generation. Before World War 1, for example, schoolchildren in Bolton could travel at special cheap fares during the summer holidays. From Monday to Friday, a 1d return fare was valid on any route for any distance; the only exception was the lengthy Horwich route, on which the fare was a princely 2d return for the 14-mile round trip, bringing within reach the delights of Lever Park or the breezy heights of Rivington Pike. To the youngster of the city streets, such glimpses could be a revelation.

56

Tramways and traffic

C. G. Harper, *The Manchester and Glasgow Road*, 1909

Traffic congestion is nothing new — only its intensity changes — and it is perhaps some consolation to our own motor age to recall that our predecessors had to grapple with the problem and were not entirely successful in their efforts to overcome it. In the early years of the 20th century, when the new electric tramways were enjoying their boom, the city of Manchester was becoming much troubled by its traffic problem, and the city council felt obliged to take action. In 1911 it appointed a sub-committee to investigate the matter. It was instructed to report on the following questions:

(a) The probable increase in tramway traffic over the next 20 years.

(b) The provisions that would be necessary in order to reduce congestion and facilitate tramway operation by the following or other means:

  (i) Widening existing streets or building new streets.

  (ii) Acquiring an 'arterial centre' for the marshalling of tramway traffic.

  (iii) The construction of subways for tramway traffic.

(c) The extent to which the financial resources of the tramways undertaking could be used for these purposes.

Supplied with information by the Tramways Department general manager, J. M McElroy, the sub-committee issued its report in 1913. This and subsequent reports provide us with a fascinating picture of the tramway system at work during this period and present some imaginative measures that could well have revolutionised the city's transport.

The general conclusion was that the basis of the problem lay in the inadequate street accommodation in the centre of the city and the poor layout of the streets. One of the effects of the resultant congestion was the low speed of services, and this in turn added to the cost of operation. As an instance, the tramways department had carried out experiments which showed that current consumption of the cars in the congested central areas was 2.26 units per car mile, whereas on a suburban part of the same route it was only 1.39 units, or nearly 40% less. It estimated that if the average speed of the cars could have been raised to 8mile/h, the saving in working expenses would have amounted to about £20,000 a year.

Measures which the department had already taken towards minimising congestion were noted. These included the provision of additional parallel routes in the central areas, and the use of Stevenson Square, Albert Square, Parker Street and George Street as termini in order to keep some of the trams out of the more congested central streets. The construction of circular routes had also served to divert come of the traffic away from the central area. On the cars

Left: Still time to amble across the road in Edwardian Manchester, but horse drawn wagons rumble over the setts amid the electric cars: the traffic problem is already in the making. Amenities of life in inner suburbs such as Openshaw include the 'Grey Mare' and the 'Penny Bazaar' — and the penny tram into town. *R. Brook*

themselves, covered tops had been introduced, thereby increasing the effective all-weather capacity of the cars and minimising the number of extras that had to be run at peak periods.

Such measures, however, could only be regarded as palliatives. Tramway traffic was continuing to increase at a substantial rate and there was no permanent means of reducing the growing amount of traffic along such thoroughfares as Oxford Road, London Road and High Street. The reduction which had recently been made in some fares (it was now possible to travel nearly three miles for one penny) had already led to a noticeable increase in the number of passengers carried, and any further reduction could be expected to have the same effect.

More drastic action inevitably came up against the question of cost; the construction of new roads and the widening of existing streets would be a costly job, as would the building of either tube railways or underground tramways. But the sub-committee stressed that other cities had faced similar problems, and it suggested that their experience should be studied with a view to seeing how far it was applicable to conditions in Manchester. Accordingly McElroy was despatched on a tour of cities in both Europe and America, including New York, Philadelphia, Boston, Chicago, Pitt-sburgh, Paris, Berlin, Vienna, London and Glasgow. On his return, in 1914, he produced his own report on what he had found and what measures could be taken in Manchester.

As background, his report included some interesting figures of the mileage of tramways in various cities in relation to their population. As an indicator of the comprehensive coverage by transport facilities, population per route-mile of tramway was taken, and this revealed that on this basis Manchester compared very favourably with most other cities, especially London.

City	Population per route-mile of tramway
Bradford	6,228
Leeds	8,196
Manchester	9,577
Sheffield	11,607
Glasgow	11,660
Liverpool	11,737
Birmingham	13,512
London	21,076

In the area served by the tramways of Manchester and Salford, the population had grown substantially during the previous 30 years; from some 800,000 in 1881 it

Left: Some of Manchester's tramway arteries carried as heavy a load as London tube railways; a line of rush-hour trams crawls along Market Street about 1910, while city authorities already grapple with the problem of congestion. *R. Brook*

Above: Covering-in the top deck was an early move to increase the all-weather carrying capacity of the tramcars. Manchester No 572, one of a hundred built in 1904-5 by Brush on 22E trucks, was soon given this 'balloon' top cover. *W. A. Camwell*

had risen to nearly 1 million in 1891, to 1.1 million in 1901 and to 1.25 million in 1911. If this rate of increase continued, the population within the next 20 years would reach just over 1.5 million. By that time, McElroy estimated, the total number of journeys per head of the population (200 in 1914) would reach 300, with the total number of passengers carried reaching at least 450 million. Looking forward for a moment, we find that in fact in 1930 the tramways of Manchester and Salford carried a total of over 400 million passengers, while in addition the buses of the two municipalities added more than another 60 million, so he was not too far out in his forecast.

Perhaps the most intriguing data included in the report concerns the traffic flows on the major arteries of the city, showing the volume of traffic carried by the trams. The numbers of passengers carried per route-mile on Manchester's principal tramway routes were given as follows:

Route	Number of passengers per route-mile per year
Stockport Road	4,486,240
Palatine Road	3,588,080
Rochdale Road	3,382,720
Oldham Road	3,315,840
Cheetham Hill Road	3,116,960
Hyde Road	3,074,720
Ashton Old Road	3,055,360

For comparative purposes figures were also provided for the traffic carried on the London 'tube' railways:

Central London	4,883,707
London Electric	4,535,475
City & South London	3,348,065
Great Northern & City	3,651,000

From these figures the remarkable fact emerged that the volume of traffic carried on three or four of Manchester's tramway routes was comparable with that carried on London's rapid transit lines, which had been constructed at much greater cost and enjoyed fully segregated right of way and complete signalling. This not only confirmed the capability of the tramway, even the conventional street routes of the type in use in

59

Manchester, but emphasised the potential for rapid transit operation in the city. It also proved that traffic congestion was not an unexpected phenomenon under such conditions!

Examining the limits to the growth of the tramway system, the report concluded that 'the ultimate volume of traffic which a tramway system can deal with is limited by the capacity of the arterial lines near the central parts of the city'. When saturation point was reached on these lines, then either further routes must be established or other transport facilities must be provided. On certain points on the Manchester system (notably London Road and Oxford Road) saturation point had almost been reached and it would be impossible to handle any signficant increase in traffic.

With regard to additional transport facilities, the range of alternatives included rapid transit lines, whether in deep level tubes, in shallow subways or on elevated structures, tramway subways in the central areas, and motorbuses. The option of rapid transit lines on elevated structures was ruled out on the grounds of unsightliness, while shallow subways were to be preferred to tubes since they were more readily accessible to passengers. The cost of such lines was tentatively estimated at around £500,000 to £700,000 a mile. 'There is no doubt', the report stated, 'that the time is rapidly drawing near when Manchester will have to be provided with rapid transit facilities, and the lines should be so laid out that they can be worked in conjunction with the surface lines'. The implication

was that any sub-surface lines should be linked with existing routes of the main line railways, a theme which was to reappear on later occasions.

While McElroy did not recommend that an underground rail system should be built at that time, he emphasised the need for any such project to be integrated with other transport modes:

'The time is not quite ripe for the immediate construction of such lines in Manchester, but it is essential that detailed consideration should be given without delay to the planning of a general scheme to be constructed later on by instalments, as developments from time to time take place.'

He was quite certain that this day would come:

'It cannot be too strongly emphasised that the future passenger transportation requirements of the city will be best met by the rapid transit system being so laid out that it can be dovetailed into the tramway system, and the two worked as a combined system'

The insistence on an integrated road and rail system is perhaps a theme more readily accepted nowadays than it was at this time.

The idea of tram subways in the central area was not favoured, in view of their high cost and their limited capacity with the operation of single cars or double units rather than full-length trains. Moreover,

60

subways would almost certainly necessitate the use of single-deck cars, which would have a lower carrying capacity than the city's standard double-deckers.

Among methods that could be put in hand to meet the more immediate needs of the situation, the first to be undertaken should be aimed at improving the tramway system. It was suggested that this should be done by the introduction of some new lines in the central area (in conjunction with new sections of road) together with the adoption of several city terminals. New lines were therefore proposed as follows:

(a) Along Aytoun Street, and a proposed new road in connection with it, to London Road at the junction with Whitworth Street.

(b) Along a proposed new road near Auburn Street, then to the junction of Chorlton Street and Whitworth Street, to Temple Street and Brunswick Street, along a proposed new road into Stockport Road.

(c) Along a new road connecting Whitworth Street with York Street, and then along York Street to Rusholme Road.

(d) Along Medlock Street from City Road to Stretford Road, then along a new road to Bradshaw Street and Princess Road.

(e) From Whitworth Street along Lower and Upper Cambridge Road to Coupland Street, with branches to Lloyd Street and Carter Street.

(f) Along a new road from the junction of Great Jackson Street and Stretford Road to Upper Moss Lane and Alexandra Road.

In conjunction with these works, it was proposed that further improvements be made in the city centre, including a new street connecting St Peter's Square with Albert Square, enabling these squares to be used as effective tram termini, and the widening of Fountain Street and Cooper Street. The services would be improved by the adoption of city termini, where cars would turn back rather than cross the city. While it was admitted that the running of cross-city services had been advantageous to the passenger, the continually growing traffic in the congested central streets was setting a limit to the number of through cars that could be satisfactorily worked. It was therefore recommended that terminal points should be employed for the working of the tramcars at the Old Infirmary site, Albert Square and St Peter's Square, High Street and Cannon Street, together with improved facilities at the existing terminus in Stevenson Square.

As a corollary to these arrangements, it was proposed that negotiations be initiated with Salford Corporation in respect of traffic coming in from that side of the city, and that a limited availability of transfer tickets be introduced to facilitate travel across the city by allowing a change of car. This would minimise the inconvenience caused by the proposed withdrawal of through services.

On the crucial question of finance for any improvement projects, the report devoted a whole section. It recognised that the matter of capital investment would affect the existing financial structure of the tramways, and that the contribution which the tramways department could make would depend on what amount of the department's profits went toward the relief of rates, as well as on the future fares policy, including any proposals for reducing fares.

In the previous year (1913) the city council had decided that the amount which the tramways department should hand over for the relief of rates should be 5% of the capital expenditure of the department. If this policy continued, the report warned, it would be impossible for the department to carry out its proposals. If the department was to improve and develop the city's transit facilities, there would have to be a limit to the amount which it handed over for rate relief, and it suggested that this should be fixed at £100,000 a year. Back in 1906 the amount had been set at £50,000, but by 1912 the figure had reached £100,000, such had been the financial success of the undertaking. Moreover, any substantial reduction in fares would have a serious effect on revenue.

Granted these provisos, McElroy's report held that the tramways department would be able to bear the cost of the proposed improvements over a number of years, to a total amount of £1 million. One further proviso it made, and that was that if the department was to be expected to contribute towards these projects, it would have to be protected against unfair competition on its routes; if necessary, further statutory powers should be obtained to make this possible. The spectre of private bus competition had as yet hardly appeared, but obviously any such practice would seriously hit the undertaking's earning capacity, as was to be amply shown in many cities during the 1920s.

In a look ahead to this rising mode of transport, the report also assessed the merit of the motorbus in the light of Manchester's need. McElroy examined a particular case to assess what might be the result if the motorbus were substituted for the tram, and his points are of especial interest in view of the motorbus policy later adopted in the city. The case in question comprised the Palatine Road and Rochdale Road routes into Manchester, which (as his figures had already shown) were among the most heavily loaded in the city. What would be the effect if these routes were to be taken over by buses?

At one point in Rochdale Road, where observations were made for the purposes of the comparison, the rush hour tram service amounted to one car every 40 seconds. If buses were employed, the service would have to be every 20 seconds, because of the smaller capacity of the bus. And in bad weather, only half the capacity of the bus would be used, since only the inside seats would be occupied (ignoring those passengers who were willing to brave the elements on the open top deck of the bus; trams already had top covers). So there would have to be a 10 second service; and this, commented the report, would practically necessitate 'a long string of omnibuses nearly the whole length of Rochdale Road from Queen's Park to town'.

It might be suggested, the report went on, that in fact not so many buses would be needed as the comparison might indicate, since the bus had a higher average speed than the tram. However, the reason for the higher speed of the bus was the fact that it took less time to load and unload at stops, since its capacity was lower. But on Rochdale Road there was a lot of through traffic, with few people alighting before the city centre was reached, and therefore it was likely that in this case the tram was operating at as high a speed as the bus would have been able to manage.

Such an illustration by no means belittled the significance of the motorbus or minimised its potential, even if this was seen as primarily complementary to the tramways. McElroy expressed his belief that motorbuses in the Manchester area would in the future form 'an important part of the surface transit facilities'. Their role would be to 'supplement the tramway services in many directions, and particularly in the outlying and thinly-populated districts, where the extension of the tramway system is rendered financially impossible owing to the heavy outlay in permanent way construction'. This was a clear recognition that the great years of tramway expansion were already over; although Manchester still went on to add to its mileage during the 1920s, the boom in construction had come to an end, primarily because of the high cost of installation which could only be justified on the most heavily-loaded routes — and these were already served.

McElroy further envisaged that buses would also operate in conjunction with the tramways in other areas, in order to improve the travelling facilities for the public (perhaps a vision of the express buses to appear in the next decade?). A valid point to be considered in relation to the introduction of buses instead of tramways was the financial benefit accruing to the city in the matter of rates and road maintenance; the tramways in 1913 had paid more than £30,000 to the city in rates in respect of the rails laid in the streets, while they also paid some £30,000 a year in maintaining about half the width of the highway in those streets, under the provisions of the Tramways Act of 1870. If buses took over, these sums would have to be found from other sources — that is, the ratepayers. Moreover, the large number of buses which would be needed to operate the services would put more wear and tear on the city streets and thus increase the cost of highway maintenance.

A final word was accorded to the trolleybus. While it was concluded that this did not have the mobility of the motorbus (an argument which figured prominently at a later stage) there might be instances where it could be of use in outlying areas, especially if its operating costs proved to be lower than those of the motorbus.

Unification of both transport services and operating authorities was urged by McElroy, in terms which have a very modern ring. He called for the creation of one central authority for the Greater Manchester area:

'It is essential that every city should have a permanent authority directing the initiation and carrying out of all schemes for new transit facilities, in order that there may be continuity of policy, and that future needs of the city and the surrounding districts over a wide area are properly looked after. It is also desirable that all the means of passenger transportation — both surface and rapid transit — should be centralised under one management'.

McElroy was also insistent on the need for integrating the different forms of transport to make the best use of each; included in his thinking were the rapid transit lines he envisaged as inevitable. In the planning of such lines, he stressed that the aim should be 'to supplement the surface transit facilities'. Rapid transit lines 'should be laid so as to follow as closely as possible the direction of the flow of the greatest volume of traffic, and the surface lines should be adapted so as to act as feeders to the rapid transit lines at all convenient points'. Though the opportunity was not to arise in respect of rapid transit lines in the Manchester area, his comments would be echoed in the thinking of later transport planners worldwide.

At this time Manchester's City Council seems to have been enjoying a plethora of reports. McElroy's was one of three presented to the Corporation, the other two being by the Watch Committee and the Improvements Committee, both of which were also concerned with similar problems. Having heard these three reports, the corporation proceeded to set up another committee, the Traffic Congestion Special Committee, in order to consider the reports and to make recommendations to the council.

This special committee duly presented its report in 1917. It agreed with the tramways committee's pro-

Above: In an attempt to obtain speedier loading and unloading at busy stops, Manchester in 1914 introduced a front-exit car, a standard four-wheeler with the platform modified to allow for a front exit under the stairs. Success of such a scheme depended on the numbers of boarding and alighting passengers being approximately equal at each stop, a situation rarely found.

Left: Corporation tramcars negotiate the junction at Mumps, Oldham, past a well-laden horse-drawn wagon carrying bales of the town's staple commodity. In the pre-motor age, slow-moving goods vehicles were blamed for adding to congestion. *R. Brook*

posals for new tramway routes in the city centre, as well as terminal points for the services, although it had doubts about one or two of the proposals. The termini were 'absolutely necessary', not only to cater for the growing tramway traffic but also to reduce congestion in the city centre. It envisaged the greater use of buses to provide central services within the inner ring of tramway termini, following the withdrawal of trams from busy thoroughfares such as Market Street, Corporation Street, Cross Street and Oldham Road. Such an idea was not too enthusiastically received; noting that nearly a thousand cars a day passed up and down Market Street, *Tramway and Railway World* commented that it was 'not explained how congestion is to be lessened by filling the streets with the larger number of omnibuses that would be required to deal with the traffic now carried by the cars'. For its part, it felt that a greater cause of congestion was the large number of horse-drawn trade vehicles using the streets.

The committee, perhaps conscious of this problem, believed that steps should be taken to provide new arterial roads to give improved access to the heart of the city. While it considered not only the tramways, but 'the possibility of other forms of passenger transport being developed in the future' in whatever form this might take, there was a crucial need for better main roads.

For the time being however, wartime conditions had eased the problem of congestion by reducing the amount of motor traffic on the roads and thereby alleviating some of the rigours of the situation. Moreover, with the likely further development of motorised transport after the war, it appeared probable that most of the horse-drawn traffic would be replaced by motor vehicles, which would be faster and more mobile and thereby result in speedier traffic flow and lessened congestion. As a result it was anticipated that the traffic problem in the more immediate future would be less than it had been before the war, and that therefore it would probably not be necessary to incur expenditure to deal with it for a number of years to come. This proved to be an over-optimistic assumption, but the committee was not alone in underestimating the rapid growth of motor transport after World War 1.

No doubt the reports were unfortunate in their timing. During the war years, little could be done to implement any of the major proposals; indeed the government refused to sanction any costly road improvements during the war. When peace returned, efforts had to be devoted to catching up on the arrears of maintenance and the lack of new equipment. By that time, costs had risen substantially, compared with prewar, making tramway development even more costly, while a major new element in the postwar scene was the motorbus, which was still something of an unknown factor when the reports were prepared.

Nevertheless Manchester still retained its faith in the tram. In a report in 1923, the new manager, Henry Mattinson (who had taken over after the death of McElroy in 1922) concluded that the motorbus could not be considered as a practicable substitute for the city's tramways. He delineated the role of each mode

Below: The new Manchester of the 1920s: suburban housing spreads southward. With its sleeper track tramway, Princess Road, Withington, in 1925 represented the start of an integrated housing and rapid transit development that never was. *R. Brook*

of transport: the motorbus where the service frequency was no more than four vehicles an hour; the trolleybus for frequencies of between four and six vehicles; and the tramcar where services of six or more vehicles an hour were required. His department's policy continued to be to develop the tramways as much as possible while using the motorbus as a feeder; in the mid-1920s the corporation had more than 800 tramcars but only about 20 buses.

During these years a regular car-building programme was pursued, while track mileage continued to grow — in the one year 1925 alone more than 8 miles were added. The new routes were especially concentrated in the expanding southern suburbs, where too a new form of construction appeared — the sleeper track. In 1924 a sub-committee of the tramways committee had been to Liverpool and Glasgow where it had seen tramways constructed on their own rights of way segregated from other traffic; returning home, it recommended the adoption of such a method of construction in Manchester.

Hence the new Princess Road, a 100ft wide dual carriageway arterial road extending southwards from the city, was provided with a 25ft central strip on which the tracks were laid on sleepers and edged with a stone kerb to separate them from the carriageways. This two-mile long line to Barlow Moor Road was completed in 1925, while a similar sleeper track followed in 1926 along another new arterial road, Kingsway, again for a distance of about two miles. Thus Manchester was beginning to get the improved roads and tramways it needed. But while the sleeper tracks were cheaper to lay and maintain than conventional paved street track, the building of new roads in which they could be integrated was limited by the high costs involved, especially in heavily built-up areas where land values were high.

On the rolling stock side, the standard type which was to serve the final three decades of the system had appeared by 1920. An all-enclosed bogie vehicle, it had 78 seats and ran on Brill type maximum-traction trucks. Already by 1920 the corporation had turned out about 50 of the new design from its own workshops, while a further 50 were on order from English Electric. During the 1920s some 350 of similar type were built, partly to replace older cars and partly to supplement the existing fleet. During these years the policy was for some 30 new bogie cars to be put into operation each year, taking over from older four-wheelers, and by the end of the 1920s the corporation's fleet included 638 bogie cars, with four-wheelers in a diminishing minority at 240.

By the later 1920s some efforts were also being directed towards improving the standard of tramway travel. These included improvements to the cars themselves; as a result of trials in 1927 Manchester decided that transverse seats should be fitted in the lower saloons of all new cars, while by 1930 some cars had been equipped with higher-speed motors which enabled them to reach 29mile/h on level track. Strategic concentration of these faster vehicles made it possible for the scheduled speed on certain routes to be raised from the overall average of 7.5 to 9mile/h. Aiding the speed-up of service was the elimination of some stops in the outer areas.

However, changes of policy were at hand. Tramcar development was soon to cease, but meanwhile in 1929 Manchester's new transport manager, R. Stuart Pilcher, and his committee produced for the council a report pointing out that the programme of constructing new bogie cars could not continue indefinitely. Two reasons were given for this. First, smaller cars were needed for operation on routes where the Corporation had running arrangements with other local authorities which used smaller four-wheelers. Second, some of Manchester's routes were more suited to the four-wheeler in view of traffic conditions. It was therefore considered that the building of large bogie cars should cease, 'at any rate for the present', and that instead it would be more useful to undertake the construction of some single-truck cars.

Pilcher therefore suggested that the next batch to be built should consist of cars 'of the single truck type of modern design'. These should have accommodation for 61 passengers, with transverse seats in the lower saloon, and be two inches wider than the standard cars. A front exit should be provided, plus a seat for the driver, and air brakes should be fitted. Platforms would be vestibuled, and the general design would 'harmonise' with the city's standard cars. It was recommended that 40 of this new design should be built, at an estimated cost of £1,800 each.

The first of the newcomers duly appeared in 1930. It certainly 'harmonised' with the established general style, as well as in details such as coloured half-lights in the saloon; the most obvious concession to modernity was the domed roof, which together with the inward slope of the body from the top deck gave a decidedly smart aspect. Built by the transport department, the body had a wooden framework, while the underframe had Duralumin sideplates, fitted with Duralumin pockets to take the body pillars. Such features contributed to the light weight of the car, which weighed only just over 11 tons compared with more than $13\frac{1}{2}$ tons for the standard bogie car. The new vehicle was mounted on a Peckham Pendulum P35 truck of 8ft 6in wheelbase fitted with two 50hp motors which served to give it a lively performance. Upholstered seats were provided for 62 passengers, while the upper saloon was even provided with electric heaters.

Two features of the original proposals were not

present: there was no front exit and there were no air brakes. Instead, the hand brake was still used for service stops, while magnetic track brakes were fitted for use on hilly routes. The report on the performance of the first arrival stated that 'it has been found that the riding of this car is very smooth and free from sidesway and that acceleration and high speed running are very satisfactory'. Sadly, the deteriorating condition of the tracks as the system declined in later years ensured that the cars did not retain the former virtues throughout their lives.

Although it had been intended that 40 of the new vehicles should be built, in the event only 38 were completed, the last of them entering service in 1932. They were destined to be the last new tramcars to be introduced in the Greater Manchester area, for already the process of contraction had begun as the motorbus proved itself to be the successful rival for the favours of the transport authorities. Final additions to other

The ultimate in Greater Manchester's tramcars: *Above:* Oldham Corporation's last new trams were a dozen built in 1926 by English Electric on 21E trucks. No 121 is seen here at Waterhead terminus.
Right: Bolton Corporation's last new cars were also by English Electric, but this time on 22E bogies. No 147 waits at the Doffcocker Inn.
Below: Manchester Corporation's last new trams were the 38 'Pullman' or 'Pilcher' cars built in 1930-32 in its own workshops on Peckham P35 trucks. No 176 stands in Hyde Road depot, showing indicators set for the 34A service to Weaste in Salford.
All: W. A. Camwell

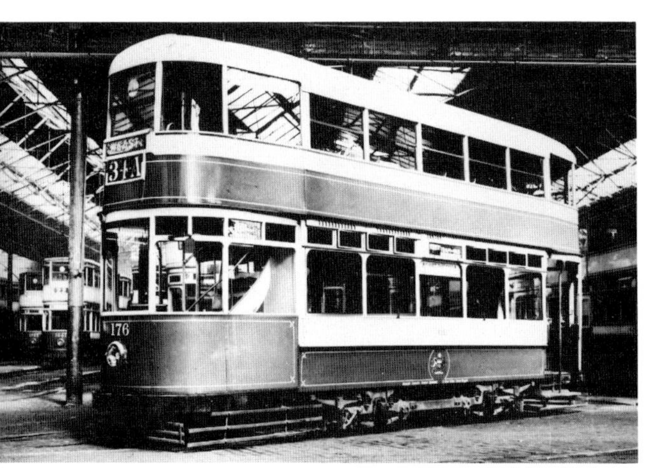

towns' car fleets were made during this decade: Ashton introduced its last new trams in 1921, Salford in 1924, Bury in 1925, Oldham in 1926, Bolton in 1927, Rochdale in 1928 and Stockport in 1929. Designs remained conventional; any new rolling stock had to be compatible, both in equipment and in operational characteristics, with earlier vehicles, many of which were more than 20 years old. New cars had to interwork with old and be maintained in the same workshops; the scope for innovation was limited. As it happened, the 'Pullmans' — or 'Pilchers' as they became known — were to outlive tramway operation in Manchester and spend their last years of active service scattered far and wide in Leeds, Sunderland, Edinburgh and Aberdeen, and it can only be wondered how far they might have foreshadowed further development in their native city.

4
Motorbus ascendant

Corporation and company

'In Manchester and the surrounding district, motor omnibuses will, in the future, form an important part of the surface-transit facilities. '

J. M. McElroy, General Manager,
Manchester Corporation Tramways, 1914

At Whitsun in 1906, Mancunians were able to sample their city's latest venture into modern transport. Taking a tramcar to the Palatine Road terminus, they could there board one of two double-deck motor omnibuses which had inaugurated a service through the pastoral fastnesses to Cheadle and Northenden. Even if nobody seriously believed it might in time replace the tramcar, the motorbus proved it could have a place in the remote suburbs, and by the outbreak of war in 1914 Manchester's motorbuses were carrying more than a million passengers a year — a tiny figure compared with the 200 million carried on the trams, but a hint of things to come. Their limited appeal to the big operator was still apparent in the accounts; the bus cost 8d a mile to run and brought in 9d a mile; while the tram cost only 7d and earned 11d.

The nature of early municipal motorbus operation was exemplified by Oldham Corporation's first service, inaugurated in 1913 between the Town Hall and The Coppice, a distance of about 1½ miles. In the first year of operation some 300,000 passengers were carried, but the route proved to be less than a goldmine; although the revenue per mile came to nearly 11d, working expenses amounted to more than 13d, an indication of the difficulties of starting a motor service which was confined to a small part of a non-bus undertaking (Oldham then had about 90 trams) and which was inevitably tucked away from the main tram-served routes. The service was withdrawn in 1919, and the two Tilling-Stevens double-deckers were sold to Warrington Corporation. Oldham reintroduced buses in 1924, and this time they survived, the first Leyland single-deckers being the precursors of a fleet which was gradually to take over from the trams. Within three years the fleet numbered more than 20, though this was still small compared with the trams which had been augmented to 120.

It was not until the later 1920s that municipal buses really began to proliferate. Bolton Corporation, which

Left: The motorbus age gets under way in Manchester. In 1906 when this photograph was taken it was still confined to the remote suburbs. Manchester Corporation No 3 is working between the Palatine Road tram terminus and Northenden.
Greater Manchester Transport, courtesy R. Dunning

had experimented with a motorbus as early as 1904, began again is earnest in 1923, the first new vehicles being single-deck Leylands; within the next five years the fleet had grown to a total of 36, including the first of the double-deckers, five Leyland Leviathans. Ashton Corporation introduced its first motorbuses in 1923 in the shape of two Guy 20-seaters, and by the end of the 1920s the fleet had expanded to 16. The first double-deckers did not come until 1932, when four Crossley Condors were added. Rochdale Corporation started to run its first buses in 1926, while Salford Corporation introduced buses on an experimental basis in 1920 to work a cross-suburban route between two tramways, while a service into Manchester was started in the following year.

A major reason for the adoption of the motorbus by the municipalities was the need to run services beyond the tram tracks, especially into new housing areas which were developing in the postwar years. But another motive was self-defence in the face of competition from the many private bus operators who flourished during this period. The effects of such competition on the municipal tramways are recalled by the SHMD Board's manager, A. G. Grundy, writing in his *Fifty Years in Transport*. Early in 1925, a local company began running motorbuses over parts of the tramway system, and it soon became evident that the board's receipts were being affected, since passengers preferred to ride in the new buses, which became known as 'the people's Rolls-Royces'.

'All we could do', writes Grundy, 'was to purchase buses and try to drive the so-called "pirates" off the

Top: Obviously proud of their new charge is the crew of this Tilling-Stevens double-decker used by Oldham Corporation on its first motorbus service in 1913. The 1½ mile long route was withdrawn in 1919.   *C. Carter*

Above: Oldham Corporation reintroduced motorbuses in 1924, when five 24-seat Leylands entered serivce. *C. Carter*

Left: Shining new and impressive for its time was the all-enclosed bodywork of Bolton Corporation's No 34, a 1928 Leyland Leviathan.   *C. Carter*

Above right: Ashton-under-Lyne Corporation introduced its first motorbus service in 1923. Loading at the Town Hall is No 41, a Guy B with 20-seat Guy body. *C. Carter*

Right: Salford Corporation began motorbus operation on an experimental basis in 1920, using this English Electric-bodied Leyland.

Bottom: 'All we could do was to purchase buses and try to drive the "pirates" off the road'. SHMD Board buses begin to take their place in the Tame Street depot alongside the austere tramcars. *W. A. Camwell*

roads'. This proved to be easier said than done before the Road Traffic Act of 1930 introduced an effective licensing system. 'Small private concerns with two or three vehicles, and correspondingly low overhead charges, were springing up like mushrooms, filching more and more of our traffic'. To counter this, the board tried cutting its fares and improving its services, but was soon obliged to introduce its own buses on one route after another. At one time, a merger of the undertaking with that of Manchester was even being considered.

As well as the municipalities and the 'pirates', three major bus rivals converged on the Greater Manchester area from north, west and south respectively: Ribble, Lancashire United, and North Western Road Car Company.

The Lancashire United Transport Company was registered in 1905 as Lancashire United Tramways to control subsidiary companies, one of which was the ambitious South Lancashire Tramways. The first motorbuses were put into service early in 1906. Motorcoach tours were started in a small way in 1914, but the Dennis vehicles were impressed into the army during the war. Operations began again after the war, and by the autumn of 1919 some two dozen vehicles were offering both short pleasure trips and extended tours.

The more prosaic side of the road business was also

During the late 1920s the independent bus operators enjoyed their heyday in providing new services between towns. In Victoria Square, Bolton, about 1928 are *above* an interesting Vulcan with dual-entrance body belonging to Belford Bus Services and operating on its route to Darwen; and *left* ready to depart for Chorley, a Leyland Tiger of Freeman's 'Silver Star' service (the 'star' can just be seen beneath the canopy). *C. Carter*

being developed. In 1920 a bus service was inaugurated between Haydock and Lowton St Mary, and thereafter rapid expansion took place, so that by the middle of the 1920s some 20 routes were in operation. Long distance and interurban services were also opened; in 1923 a daily express service to Blackpool was started at a fare of 4s (20p) single, while a day return was available at the bargain price of 5s (25p). By 1927 there were services from Manchester to both Liverpool and Southport. If you did not want to go so far afield, for an evening out you could get a combined bus and theatre ticket enabling you to travel by bus into Leigh to see a show from the grand circle at an inclusive charge of 1s 6d (7½p).

Ribble Motor Services was established in 1919 and in time expanded to cover a large area of Lancashire, from Liverpool to the Lake District, partly through amalgamation and absorption of small operators. It developed services from the north into Manchester; for example, express buses came in from Blackburn, Burnley, Colne, Accrington and Clitheroe. In the southern part of the Greater Manchester area, the North Western Road Car Company was formed in 1923 on the basis of the Peak District Committee, a branch of British Automobile Traction, which had begun operations in Macclesfield in 1913. The new company set up its headquarters in Stockport, where its predecessor had already come to terms with the corporation.

By the end of the 1920s the main line railway companies were also extending their road transport interests, following their newly acquired powers under the Railways (Road Transport) Acts of 1928, and railway-operated services were appearing on many roads. An example from 1929 was the Manchester-

Above: One of the larger bus operators to develop during the 1920s was the North Western Road Car Company, working services southward from Manchester into Cheshire and Derbyshire. *Ian Allan Library*

Above right: Luxury in the new age of long-distance road travel: 'Manchester and London Direct' is offered by Fingland's Services in this Duple-bodied AEC Regal of 1933. *Ian Allan Library*

Sheffield route started by the LNER and the LMS, using AEC and Thornycroft vehicles making six journeys a day; with 14 stops on the way, they took just over two hours, for which the fare was 3s 8d single (18p) and 5s 10d return (29p).

Thoughts of some kind of agreement between the local undertakings and the railway companies, on the lines of the arrangements made on the other side of the Pennines in Sheffield and Huddersfield, were aired in Lancashire from time to time, but nothing materialised. The railway companies were soon to give up their direct operation of bus services, preferring instead to take a share in established businesses.

With the growth in motor transport in the 1920s and 1930s the railways were losing their monopoly of pleasure traffic. Once the natural way to go from Manchester to Blackpool was by train from Victoria, but by about 1912 motorbuses and charabancs were already taking trippers to the seaside. The war caused a hiatus, but afterwards the trade resumed and grew vigorously. In the early postwar period you could take a day return from Manchester to Blackpool for 13s (65p) or if you were going on a week's holiday you could get a period return for 17s 6d (87½p). Demand

at peak times sometimes exceeded supply, and road hauliers fitted their vehicles with detachable bodies, carrying goods during the week and then switching to 'chara' bodies at the weekend for the seaside runs. Under such conditions the small operator flourished, buying his vehicle and entering the business with the minimum of formality, since regulation was almost non-existent before the 1930 Road Traffic Act; this was the era of unrestrained competition in road transport operations. You could enjoy a trip from Manchester to Blackpool and back for 4s 6d or 5s ($22\frac{1}{2}$p or 25p) and sometimes even as little as 3s 6d ($17\frac{1}{2}$p), which was fair value for a round journey of about 100 miles, even if the condition of the vehicle could not be guaranteed, any more than the return time — or the return at all that same night.

Apart from such pleasure traffic, road services were also providing links across the country for business and other serious travel. For example, by the end of the 1920s Manchester had regular services to and from Birmingham and London. North Western and Midland Red jointly started running between Manchester and London via Coventry and Birmingham on 2 August 1929 from Manchester, with the first trip from London the next day. Departures were every day (including Sunday) from London at 8.30am, reaching Manchester at about 7pm, while from Manchester departure was at 8.45am with arrival in London scheduled for around 7pm. The through fare was 15s single (75p) and 25s return (£1.25). In addition a daily journey was made between Manchester and Birmingham, departing from Manchester at 4pm and from Birmingham at 9am and taking about four hours.

An important step in the growth of long-distance road services was the setting up of the Limited Stop Pool. Started on an experimental basis in 1928, and so successful that it was expanded in 1929, the Pool operated services between Liverpool, Manchester, Leeds and Newcastle. North Western joined the partners Northern General, West Yorkshire and Yorkshire Woollen District, while Lancashire United became a member in 1932.

Proof of the potential of the bus, as well as the merits of coordination rather than competition, found expression in the evolution of the express bus operations which became a feature of Greater Manchester's transport facilities. The inspiration for express buses went back at least to 1924, when the Manchester Tramways Committee adopted a scheme to run such a service between St Peter's Square and Didsbury, making intermediate stops only at Fallowfield and Withington. A 20min frequency was planned, with a fare for the through journey of 6d ($2\frac{1}{2}$p). But the real breakthrough came in 1927 with the inauguration on 1 April of what was quickly to become a network of fast long-distance bus services crossing the city and extending along the tram routes and beyond, to give a new coordinated system across the region.

It was believed to be the first network of its kind in the world where express bus services were operated in parallel with principal tramways. Along the tram routes the buses stopped only at the fare stages, which were about $\frac{3}{4}$ mile apart, and the fares were double those on the trams, with a minimum of 2d. Buses were extended beyond the tram termini, linking existing services into the outer areas, and along these roads they operated in the normal way.

One of the aims of the scheme was, in the words of the tramways department, 'to afford an indication as

Above: For the initiation of the limited-stop express services which started in 1927, Manchester Corporation employed a fleet of single-deckers. This Associated Daimler 32-seater, photographed on Kingsway when new in January 1928, shows the indication 'Gatley' but the side destination boards have not yet been fitted. The body has the characteristic cutaway rear entrance, and offered a standard of comfort superior to the tramcar. *Greater Manchester Transport, courtesy R. Dunning*

to the willingness of the public to pay more for journeys of greater comfort and expedition' than on the tramcars. It was not envisaged that the new services would materially reduce the traffic on the tramways, where the 1d fare was still the most used, but that it would provide faster journeys over the longer distance. Also in mind was the more affluent commuter from the farther suburbs; it was hoped that he might be attracted to take a fast and comfortable bus rather than use his own car for his daily journeys, thus helping to alleviate traffic congestion in the city.

The new express buses proved to be an instant success, with results exceeding the expectations of the department. Mainstay of the services were 32-seat single-deckers of Associated Daimler and Bristol manufacture, offering a higher standard of comfort and speed than the trams. The smaller vehicle gave a more select atmosphere for those who wanted to avoid the seething masses on the prolaterian tramcars.

But it was not enough to confine the scheme to Manchester's own tram routes, where it would inevitably abstract traffic from the older and slower mode of transport. It needed to spread farther afield. Flushed with success, Manchester negotiated with its neighbouring operators and got their co-operation in a wider scheme which sent buses hurrying from one side of the city to the other. Local authorities brought in were Salford, Bury, Oldham, Rochdale, Ashton, Heywood, Bolton, the SHMD and Stockport, while the South Lancashire company was also involved. Arrangements were put in hand for six routes, all of them operating across Manchester: Bolton-Hyde, Bury-Stockport, Heywood-Gatley, Rochdale-Altrincham, Oldham-Urmston, and Stalybridge-Eccles. By early 1928 the 6 routes had grown to 16,

Below: One for the album: Driver Woodhouse stands beside his Manchester single-deck Leyland No 29 about 1930. Operating on service 10 between Greenfield and Piccadilly, No 29 carries the 'Limited Stop' headboard. *Greater Manchester Transport, courtesy R. Dunning*

and new buses were on order to enable the frequencies to be increased as this became necessary; in fact, so popular were some services that the initial half-hourly headway was soon narrowed to 15 or 20min, and even to 5min at peak times.

Fares at first were double those on the trams over the tramway routes in order to give some protection and to keep shorter-distance passengers off the buses. In 1928 day return tickets were being issued at the rate of a single fare and a half on journeys where the ordinary single fare was 6d (2½p) or more, thus encouraging the daily traveller or the shopper to come into Manchester from a wide area around.

By 1930 there were 27 services, operating not only between the major towns but far into the outer suburbs and the surrounding countryside. Unlikely linkings resulted from operational convenience and the avoidance of layover time in the city centre, giving some lengthy routes; from Gatley in the southern outskirts, for example, through Manchester to Norden,

further stimulated the changes, increasing the momentum of the outward movement.

Success of the bus network proved that it was practicable for a number of different operators to work together to provide an integrated system. This had, of course, been demonstrated in the heyday of the tram, but here was now a much more extensive illustration of the fact. Partly it was a measure of self-defence

Below: Bus services were superimposed on the tramways, to offer faster travel between towns. Here at Hollinwood the bus makes a through journey (the 'Bus Stop Express' sign can be seen on the right) while Manchester and Oldham trams stand back to back each side of the boundary before returning to their respective home towns. *W. A. Camwell*

north of Heywood, was a distance of about 18 miles, from Hyde to Bolton was about 17 miles, and from Altrincham to Littleborough via Rochdale, more than 20 miles. In conjunction with the company operators, routes also radiated from Manchester to Hayfield, Buxton and Macclesfield.

The new network reflected the changing transport needs of a region in which the distribution of population and industry was changing. The tramway system, virtually completed 20 or 30 years earlier, had not kept pace; it had been outgrown. Moreover, the buses

against the intrusion of independents and 'pirates' as well as a move to cater for the needs of an expanding area, but it was nevertheless a convincing demonstration of the merits of coordination, a fact not without relevance to the protracted discussions on the possibility of an area transport board. Also germane to this question were the administrative problems involved in the smooth running of a network shared by a dozen operators: how many man-hours had to be spent in devising schedules to suit everyone concerned, and in calculating how much of the proceeds went to

75

each? The Bolton-Salford-Manchester-Hyde service, for example, was worked by five different operators: Lancashire United, Bolton, Salford, Manchester, and the SHMD Board.

A basic shortcoming of the tramways was also highlighted: they were inadequate to cater for the longer-distance traffic. There was no way of operating a fast tram service; since a faster car could not overtake another to offer a quicker service, the speed along a route was that of the slowest car. Thus cars entering Manchester from the outer suburbs or adjoining towns had a lengthy journey time, with a speed that decreased as they neared the central area where more services converged on to the same tracks. Speed was restricted to that of the slowest car stopping at all the stops to handle the short-distance traffic. The express bus could overtake a stopping bus on the same route and could also work 'limited stop' in the inner area, thus maintaining a faster schedule.

In effect the buses were providing a superior class of service. With higher fares and better speed and comfort, they became the 'first class' mode of transport, while the old trams were relegated to 'second class'. The distinction was heightened by the fact that the buses served new residential areas while the trams were largely confined to the older and predominantly proletarian districts. No doubt Engels would have nodded knowingly if he could have seen the fast buses bringing in the affluent outer-suburban commuters; back in 1844 he had noted that the 'members of the money aristocracy can take the shortest road through the middle of all the labouring districts to their places of business, without ever seeing that they are in the midst of the grimy misery that lurks to the right and the left'.

Operation of this cross-city bus network was frowned upon by the new Area Traffic Commissioners set up under the Road Traffic Act of 1930. Under the Act the licensing of public service vehicles was taken away from the local authorities and placed in the hands of the Commissioners, who had discretion to issue licences as they thought necessary to meet local requirements. Now in their view these fast buses crisscrossing the central areas of Manchester, mingling with other buses and with tramcars, as well as the increasing amount of motor traffic, were a factor in adding to congestion.

Ironically the demise of the trams was to contribute to the phasing out of the express services. Up to now the buses had been operating as supplementary to the trams along the same routes, offering the faster and more expensive option. But what happened when the trams came to be replaced by buses? Was there any justification in having two different categories of the same type of vehicle along the same route? There was not; hence the obvious move was to discontinue the express services along the tram routes as they were converted, thus returning to only one standard of service. The replacing bus may have been faster than the tram it replaced, but since it had to stop at all the old tram stops, it was slower than the express bus. In such cases a lower standard had to be accepted; perhaps it was more democratic to revert to one class for all.

Limited stop services were given increased emphasis after the war, with the need for economical operation of the longer-distance services which had grown in importance. Combined with careful scheduling, they enabled the best use to be made of a given number of vehicles, especially in peak periods, while offering the added inducement of speed to the outer suburban commuter.

Left: The newly-appointed Traffic Commissioners did not take kindly to the limited stop buses which they claimed added to congestion in the city centre; here one of the single-deckers makes its way through Manchester's traffic. *R. Brook*

The road to Wythenshawe

'The Corporation building estates, with their row upon row of little red houses, are a regular feature of the outskirts of the industrial towns. The expense of getting to and from town is one of the more obvious problems of rehousing.'

George Orwell,
The Road to Wigan Pier, 1937

If the 'expresses' marked one stage in the ascent of the motorbus, no less symbolic was its victory at Manchester's 'country estate' at Wythenshawe. Tramway expansion in Manchester still seemed within the realms of possibility up to 1929 when the City Council approved a recommendation by the tramways committee for a scheme to extend Princess Road from Barlow Moor Road to the Stockport-Altrincham road at Wythenshawe, a distance of about two miles, provision being made for the tramway to be laid on sleeper track and to be carried on a bridge over the Mersey at Northenden. The cost was put at £50,000 and a service of express cars was envisaged. An amendment in council that the proposal should be 'referred back' to the committee on the grounds that tramways were 'passing out' was defeated, though the mover of the amendment was nearer the truth than he might have realised.

Wythenshawe was Manchester's great Utopia, the Hampstead Garden Suburb of the North. The old Manchester was over-crowded; large areas had grown up during the Industrial Revolution, leaving a legacy of rows of closely packed terrace houses which lacked the amenities of modern life. These densely-built streets had advantages for the tramways; they provided a high concentration of traffic within a fairly limited area, where large numbers of people travelled short distances. But it was not so good for the people who had to live in such conditions. The only way to improve their lot was to build new houses to replace the old, and these new houses were not only to be of a better standard but were also to be less densely packed so that there was room for gardens and other open spaces. This in turn meant that more land was needed, since there was just not enough land within the old city bounds to rehouse all the people in the new more dispersed style. The problem for Manchester was that it was hemmed in on nearly all sides by other towns and built-up areas; there was only one way in which the city could expand to find the space it needed, and that was southward, towards the wide pastures of Cheshire. And in that direction lay Manchester's new town.

Situated six to seven miles to the south of the city, Wythenshawe was beyond the new suburbs that were

Left: The road to Wythenshawe: suburban housing and youthful trees. The motorbus provides the means of transport; here in Brownley Road a corporation double-decker is overtaken by an airport bus on its way to Ringway, no less symbolic of the new era in transport.
City of Manchester Local History Library

Right: Wythenshawe: the wide open spaces of grassland and trees. The bus has to travel further to gather in a useful load, while a younger generation finds the bicycle an alternative means of transport. This is Findon Road, Baguley.
City of Manchester Local History Library

Below: The new suburbia for the masses: Council housing on Manchester's Wilbraham Estate at Lloyd Street, along which the tramway was extended in 1924. Population density was much lower, hence loading on the trams was less concentrated. Rents were higher, journey times longer and fares higher; transport had to subsidise new suburban living.   *R. Brook*

already spreading this way. In 1926 Manchester bought an extensive tract of land for a new town designed to accommodate up to 100,000 people in order to take the pressure off the old central areas, and it was here that building was soon under way.

A report by the new tramways manager, Stuart Pilcher, who took over in 1929, came out against extending the tramways. He pointed out that the service to the new area would be better provided by buses; in view of the distance of Wythenshawe from the city centre, the journey would be faster by bus. The department was already operating express bus services for routes of this length and these had been proving a success. It would be wasteful to indulge in the construction of new tramways if express buses were to be run parallel with them.

As to the idea that trams could offer cheaper fares, he believed this would not stand up to scrutiny in a particular case such as this. The proposed extension would be expensive to construct, and would put an extra financial load on the rest of the tramways which were already sufficiently burdened. If it was held that special low fares should be conceded to the inhabitants of such areas as Wythenshawe, then these could just as well be given on the buses. The use of buses would involve no such costly work as road widening or the reconstruction of bridges. Moreover, as the estate developed and transport facilities were required away from the main highways and on roads further into the estate, such services could easily be provided by buses without the installation of the fixed equipment needed for tramways. The choice of buses would obviate the financial risk that would be incurred with tramways as traffic demands changed.

Recent developments in the motorbus, Pilcher claimed, proved that it was quite competent to handle the traffic to and from such districts as Wythenshawe, even with the expected increase in passenger loads that

would result as the estate developed. He reminded the council that there was no adequate protection for the corporation's services outside the municipal boundaries (and Wythenshawe was not brought within Manchester's boundaries until 1930) so that any tramways extending outside that area could be at risk from competition from other operators.

For the transport department the development of Wythenshawe raised problems. While the intention was that work should be provided in the new town so that people could find employment near their suburban residences, this principle proved impossible to realise in full. Most of the new inhabitants still had jobs near their old homes, so they needed transport to carry them between home and work. This involved them in extra expense. They were already having to pay higher rents; new council house rents were typically twice what tenants had been paying in their old homes, and a rise from 7s or 9s a week (35-45p) to between 13s and 15s (65-75p) was a not inconsiderable item when a typical wage was only £2.50 or £3 a week. If on top of this they had to pay out a further considerable sum on daily bus fares to get to and from work, they could be worse off in spite of the pleasanter living conditions, while some people might well be deterred from moving out altogether.

This proved to be one of the perennial problems of the rehousing programmes that many councils were undertaking during this interwar period. One measure adopted to alleviate the hardship of extra travelling expense was to supply cheap transport, with sub-sidised fares, and this was done in Manchester where the Wythenshawe buses operated at specially low fares comparable with the trams. Between the estate and the city, the return bus fare was 8d (about $3\frac{1}{2}$p). Though in line with the municipal objective of providing transport at the lowest possible cost to the citizen (as McElroy had enunciated years before) this policy was open to controversy. Why, it was argued, should one section of the community be subsidised in this manner at the expense of other users of the transport services?

As late as 1946 Manchester Corporation found itself rebuked by the North Western Area Traffic Commissioners, who in effect pointed out that it was inequitable that the travelling public in general should have to subsidise one section of the community. The fares to and from Wythenshawe should be put on the same basis as the rest of the city's bus fares. If there was a case for subsidising some passengers, the Com-missioners declared, then this should not be done by means of the municipal transport department.

Nor was this the only problem for the department. New housing estates such as Wythenshawe which were at a distance of several miles from the city centre, involved lengthy journeys. This not only took the passenger's time, but from the department's point of view it meant that long runs were being made at sub-standard fares, so tying up buses for considerable periods of time during which they were prevented from being employed on more remunerative services. Moreover, since the journey to and from town took up much of the rush hour, the buses were unable to make more than one out-and-back journey; and that one journey was made loaded with cheap-fare passengers travelling all the way, so that few more profitable fares could be picked up en route.

Nor were the estates always conducive to the most economic operation. The new housing was built to a much lower density than the old; there were about 12 houses to the acre, providing accommodation for some 50 to 60 people in this area, which was pleasantly laid out with gardens and open spaces in the approved style. This contrasted with the old urban housing of the late 19th century; this had managed to cram in as many as 50 houses to the acre, where some 250 people might be living. Certainly the new conditions were better for the inhabitants concerned, but they meant that the 'catchment' for public transport was more widely spread and that any individual route offered a much smaller patronage. The suburban buses were having to travel further to gather in useful loads. It was little wonder that Pilcher did not favour extending costly tramways.

The concept of Wythenshawe included 'Parkways', which were described as 'landscaped roads running through wedges of green space between strips of urban development', a description calculated to cause dismay to bus operators seeking economic routes. The idea seems to have been adapted from an earlier vision by Ebenezer Howard for electric railways along the main roads, although the project as originally planned was not completed. Although such roads might take through traffic, they were not necessarily the best layout for the running of local transport services, which often had to depart from the Parkways to serve the various developing housing districts along tortuous suburban roads which added more to operating mileage than to productive revenue.

Estates such as Wythenshawe represented one part of the spread into Cheshire, as the suburbs crept steadily southward to open up new homelands for the folk of the big city. The result was a change in the transport pattern, from a close mesh of comparatively short densely-trafficked routes to a more open network of longer routes. The transformation of North Cheshire was one of the phenomena of the period, with villages and towns in the tranquil countryside being turned into dormitory suburbs for Mancunians. The population of the areas under the influence of the Manchester overflow grew by nearly 40% during the 1920s and by almost another 50% in the 1930s and

1940s. This growth was essentially a product of the motor age: the private car for the wealthy, the bus for the mass of people who had moved out to the new residential areas and commuted daily.

For the transport department there was another side to this movement. While the population was spreading itself more thinly across sprawling suburbs, at the same time the population in the older inner areas was declining. Referring to this trend, Pilcher pointed out in 1938 that in only six years the population in the 24 inner wards within two miles of Manchester's centre had decreased by more than 50,000, while during the same period the population in the 12 outer wards had increased by over 45,000. Thus the central areas were losing their population; the implication for the transport department was obvious. The older central areas were especially the domain of the tramways, which had carried the densest traffic at the penny fares which had stimulated the great mass movement of the city's people. Now their traffic was falling to an extent that was putting their future viability into question. Could their renewal be justified if the trend continued, as it appeared likely to? And could they make the profits that made it possible to subsidise cheap fares?

So no further extensions were made; the golden age of the Manchester tramcar was over by the end of the 1920s. Two other proposals for sleeper track tramways were also abandoned: along Mauldeth Road West from the Princess Road sleeper track to Barlow Moor Road, and along Broadway in Moston. In both cases the road layout provided for the construction of a tramway in the central reservation, but powers were not sought for the lines and it was agreed that the

schemes should be dropped. In 1929 the city decided on a curtailment of expenditure on track and cars, promoted a Bill which included powers to run buses or trolleybuses on all its tram routes, and significantly changed the title of the Tramways Department to *Transport* Department.

Though it still remained to be proved that the tram could be effectively replaced by the bus, this was soon to be done in the case of one of the city's most renowned routes, the 'Circular'. In July 1929 the committee recommended to the city council that the 53 route be replaced by buses. The '53' had a character all its own, on two counts: its topography and its cars. While most routes quite naturally ran between city and suburb, the 53 never ventured into the centre of Manchester at all; instead it made almost a circle (hence almost but not quite justifying its description of 'Circular') around the inner suburbs at a radius of about two miles from the centre. It started up in Queens Road, Hightown, headed away from the city for a distance, then turned to cross the main Rochdale and Oldham roads, ploughed on through older densely-populated districts to cross both Ashton New Road and Ashton Old Road, to meet the Denton route at Belle Vue. Thence it disappeared round the corner, and went on to cross the Stockport road, continued through the suburbs of Longsight and Rusholme, then negotiated an extensive one-way loop to reach its terminus at Brooks's Bar, only about three miles as the crow flies from its starting point.

During its journey of some eight miles, the 53 thus crossed a good half dozen of the main radial routes, and so formed a valuable connecting link between one

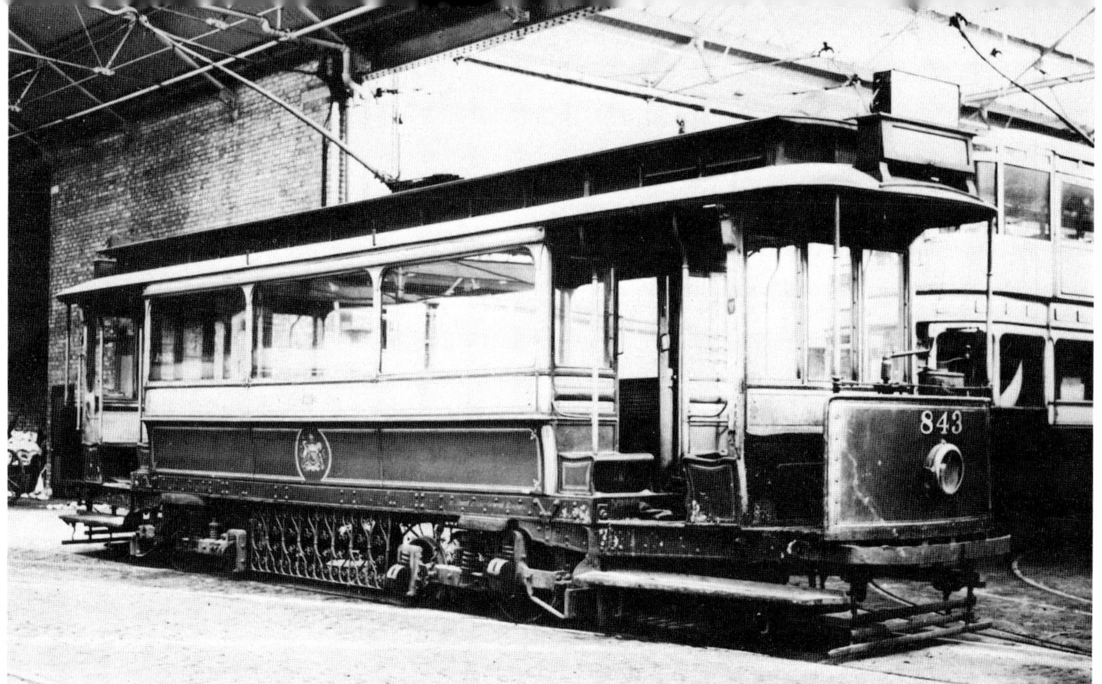

Above left: End of the line for the trams: the East Didsbury terminus of the 2-mile long Kingsway sleeper track.   *W. A. Camwell*

Above: One of the distinctive 'California' type combination cars used on Manchester's 53 route until 1930. Seen in Birchfields Road depot in 1938, No 843 has since been restored to operate on the Heaton Park museum line.   *W. A. Camwell*

and another. Its disadvantage was that it had to negotiate a succession of junctions, where it not only encountered other services but also had to cross flows of traffic along the main roads, all potential sources of disruption to the schedules. Not only had cars to endure the continual wear and tear occasioned by bumping over the many junctions, but there were also numerous sections of single track which could cause further delays. The route not only militated against speedy operation, but the fact that it mostly traversed tracks unused by other services made it a suitable candidate for conversion.

The case was strengthened by the non-standard nature of the rolling stock, which was quite unlike that used on the rest of the city's lines. Because of low bridges, the 53 employed single-deckers — not ordinary ones, but what were known as the 'California' type, though why a design adapted for use in the sunny climes of the Western United States should have been thought desirable in the inclemencies of Manchester's weather remains something of a mystery. The saloon was flanked by lengthy open plat-

forms, on which seats were provided, so that a good proportion of the passengers could enjoy the fresh air of Forge Lane and Moss Side. Operations required a stock of about 70 of these cars, some of which dated back to 1903. As fate would have it, the only surviving Manchester tram is one of this type; beautifully restored to its original condition, it now runs in Heaton Park.

Under the circumstances peculiar to itself, the 53 was therefore considered ripe for conversion to motorbus operation. Double-deck buses could be employed (the newly-developed lowbridge double-decker could get under the bridges that would not clear a double-deck tram) and the seating capacity would be higher. Buses would not be delayed by waiting at passing places, while they could speedily traverse the junctions with other routes without being held up and without the pounding of steel wheels over points and crossings. From the passenger's point of view, the new vehicles would provide a better standard of comfort, with enclosed accommodation in all weathers, plus upholstered seats.

So for Manchester's first big conversion, a fleet of low bridge double-deckers was obtained, comprising Crossleys and Leyland Titans with Strachans and Crossley bodies, in which 'passengers are carried in surroundings of great comfort', as one contemporary described it. Each bus seated 50 passengers, compared with 40 on the trams. The first buses went into service on 3 March 1930, the new vehicles being gradually introduced until they took over completely from 7 April. The contrast was striking: the old trams showed up badly beside their successors, while the

Left: In the new era of the municipal double-deck bus, Rochdale Corporation completed the changeover from trams between 1930 and 1932; No 78 was a balcony double-decker built by English Electric on 21E truck in 1920.

Below right: Rochdale Corporation's first double-deck bus, a 1930 Crossley Condor with lowbridge Crossley body, presaged the arrival of numerous Condors to replace trams. *C. Carter*

standard of service and comfort was clearly greatly enhanced. On their cushioned seats the passengers could laugh at the weather and not even notice the crossing of one route over another where the trams had crashed over the points, while the service was unhindered by delays on single track.

Results of the first year's working justified the department's optimism. An additional 2.4 million passengers had been carried, an increase of 11% compared with the last year of the trams. The average speed of the service had risen from 9mile/h to 11mile/h. The financial figures were no less encouraging; the trams had cost 17.37d per car-mile to operate, while revenue had been only 16.731d, resulting in a loss per car-mile of 0.639d, which added up to a deficit on the year of £4,285. The buses, on the other hand, had turned this round into a useful profit; their costs were only 13.040d per vehicle-mile, while they earned 17.15d per mile, resulting in a surplus per mile of about 4d and a profit on the year's operations of £25,255. The changeover was thus triumphantly vindicated, even if the special local factors of the case did not necessarily appear to make it universally valid.

The effect of express bus services on the tramways was illustrated in the case of the lengthy Altrincham route, on which there was also competition from the unlicensed buses of private operators. The corporation found that tramway receipts had fallen as bus receipts had risen. 'The public evidently prefer the omnibuses, and are prepared to pay higher fares to travel in them',

Pilcher concluded in 1930 when he recommended that the service be taken over entirely by buses. With the added argument that a sum of nearly £100,000 would be needed for the reconstruction of the tramway if it were to be retained, the change appeared inevitable. At the time the through tram fare from the city was only 4d (less than 2p) for a distance of more than nine miles, and it was anticipated that this would have to be raised when the buses took over; it may be wondered how many passengers took advantage of this low fare in view of the faster buses, as well as the frequent train service on the paralleling Manchester South Junction & Altrincham Railway, soon to be improved with electrification. Accordingly the trams were withdrawn in 1931.

Manchester was not alone in going in for change. Rochdale, for example, had decided that the motorbus was better suited to its needs, and a two-year conversion programme ended with the running of the town's last trams on 12 November 1932. Among factors influencing the decision were the costs of replacing obsolete equipment and the low traffic density on some of the routes. But the change emphasised another aspect of the transformation: the fact that no undertaking, indeed no single route, could be considered in isolation. A through service was operated between Manchester and Rochdale by the cars of the two corporations, and while Rochdale had withdrawn all its own trams, Manchester was still operating trams within its own area.

The introduction of the new through bus service therefore took some of the traffic off the tracks that were still in use, with the result that the remaining trams had to bear an increasing proportion of fixed costs. Moreover, the new buses were paralleling the trams on the Manchester part of the route, thus intensifying congestion on these roads. It was the worst of both worlds, so it was not surprising that the remaining trams still running over the tracks should have their future called into question.

The case was strengthened by the success claimed for the new buses; whereas the Manchester-Rochdale trams had operated at a loss, the buses were found to be turning in a profit. Speeds were also increased; whereas the trams had averaged only 9.55mile/h, the buses attained just over 11mile/h, resulting in a reduction of 15% on a journey of 65min. Again, the sad fact was that the tram could not operate so fast on a route where it had to encounter the slower local services running on the same tracks.

With the apparent success in mind, in 1933 the Manchester City Council approved the replacement of the trams still operating on the Rochdale Road services. These comprised not only the relevant part of the former joint route, but about 13 miles of routes serving Middleton, Heywood, Heaton Park, Blackley and Conran Street. The tracks were reported to be in urgent need of renewal, particularly at the inner ends of the routes where the heaviest traffic had always been concentrated. The cost of renewal was put at more than £8,000 per mile of track, so that the total sum involved, including the renewal of junctions, would be some £220,000. This sum of money was just not available to the transport department. The renewal fund was already seriously depleted; it stood at only £231,000, of which £117,000 had been earmarked for the purchase of buses, leaving only £114,000 available for the whole of the undertaking.

Further, continuation of tramway operation would require the purchase of new cars to replace old. Of the total of 835 tramcars then in stock (the department also now had 350 buses), some 150 were of the old four-wheel type; 120 of these were 30 years old, while many others were 20 to 25 years old. Although the changeover from tram to bus had so far resulted in the withdrawal of 180 old cars, many of the elderly four-wheelers still had to be retained in action. Up to this time, about 21 miles of track had been abandoned, thus saving the costs of renewal which would have amounted to £165,000. Moreover, it was stressed, in every case conversion had resulted in an increase in revenue, averaging 0.42d per mile worked, and in the year 1932-33 the buses had turned in a profit of nearly £12,000. Accordingly, the new scheme went ahead; the first part came into effect when buses took over the Heywood service on 2 May 1934, followed by Middleton on 25 March 1935. The process of eliminating the tram was now well under way.

Transformation

'In the case of large undertakings, there is usually room for both trams and buses.'
R. Stuart Pilcher, *Road Passenger Transport*, 1937

A comparison of tram and bus operations in Manchester in 1930 reveals the relative roles of the two forms of transport at the start of this decisive decade. The trams were still very much in the premier position; they numbered more than 900 against fewer than 200 buses, and they were carrying more than 300 million passengers a year compared with only about 30 million on the buses. The concentration of traffic is shown by the fact that the tramway route-mileage was substantially less than the bus route-mileage: 160 miles against more than 200. The bus mileage of course included many less heavily-trafficked suburban routes while the trams traditionally served the densely-loaded shorter-distance routes, on which they offered lower fares. On the trams the average fare per mile was little more than 0.5d while on the buses it was over 1d. The higher load factor on the trams was seen in the average number of passengers carried per vehicle per mile: 13, against only 5 on the buses (for comparison, it is interesting to note that the average for buses of the passenger transport executives in 1980 was 6).

By 1939 the position had been transformed. The tramcar fleet had been practically halved to about 470, while the number of buses had almost quadrupled to reach nearly 800, The number of passengers carried by tram had more than halved, while bus passengers had increased sevenfold to over 200 million. Nor was the change confined to Manchester itself; the accompanying table indicates the rise in importance of the municipal bus throughout the conurbation during the 1930s. Between 1931 and 1938 the number of buses owned by a dozen municipal operators more than doubled in total.

Below: The new municipal transport at the end of the 1920s: Bury Corporation AEC Regent No 27, with front-exit body, turns at Whitefield Station. The station sign announces 'Trains to Manchester and Bury Every Few Minutes': coordination or competition?   *C. Carter*

The Rise of the municipal motorbus in Greater Manchester

	First motor bus	1931		1938	
		Number of buses	Passengers carried (millions)	Number of buses	Passengers carried (millions)
Ashton	1923	21	5.2	32	13.7
Bolton	1904*	59	NA	127	NA
Bury	1925	30	7.2	71	18.9
Leigh	1920	29	4.1	41	9.2
Manchester	1906*	258	56.5	645	173.8
Oldham	1913*	56	12.2	166	38.3
Ramsbottom	1923	13	1.7	35	2.5
Rochdale	1926	54	9.9	118	37.1
Salford	1920	94	17.2	181	51.0
SHMD	1925	54	12.3	68	16.7
Stockport	1919	55	10.1	77	16.3
Wigan	1919	78	13.9	102	29.1

*Experimental services

Growth in Manchester Corporation's bus fleet from the end of the 1920s was particularly influenced by

Above: Symbol of a city: Manchester Corporation's Crossley Mancunian of 1934 brought a characteristic 'look' to the growing bus fleet. No 429 stands in Piccadilly in 1935. The private cars also recall the increasing problem of traffic congestion. *G. H. F. Atkins*

two factors: the development of the longer-distance network, and then the accelerating replacement of the tramways. Among the expanding fleet, not surprisingly the local builder Crossley, as well as the not-too-distant Leyland, figured prominently in the supply of vehicles.

Although the Crossley company had had its origins in the production of gas engines and had started producing motorcars in 1906, it was not until 1928 that it began the production of buses. Eagle single-deckers supplied to Manchester in 1929 were described as 'eminently serviceable' for either light city service or interurban operation, while their 32-seat bodies were 'particularly appreciated on account of the comfort of the semi-bucket seats and the efficient ventilation'. The year 1930 saw the delivery to Manchester Corporation of the first Alpha single-deckers and the Condor double-decker. The Crossley works at Gorton was well placed to supply what was to become a big customer, but it was not alone in the field, for in the same year there was an intake of Leylands, both Titan TD1s and Tigers. The total of 60 lowbridge double-deckers entered service on the 'test case' route, the 53, where they were hailed as the naturally superior form of transport.

Many more Condors followed, including another 70 in 1931, 40 in 1932, and some 65 in 1933-34. The first of the highbridge pattern appeared in 1931 now that double-deckers were spreading to routes unencumbered by restrictive bridges.

An important landmark was the introduction of the diesel engine. After trials during the year, on 13 December 1930 a Crossley with a Gardner diesel engine was put into service on the 53 route, and as a result an order for five more was placed in 1931, by which time Crossley had the diesel-engined bus in full production. The performance of the diesel bus was reported as excellent and encouraging; on its tests it established a reputation for running to time, while its fuel consumption on a straight run was 14 miles to the gallon, using oil costing only 4d (about 2p) a gallon, compared with its petrol-engined equivalent which did only 5 miles to the gallon and used fuel costing 1s (5p) a gallon. The maker claimed that the use of the diesel could result in a saving of at least £300 a year per bus. With the growing fleet, such figures were not to be disregarded, while they helped to give further impetus to the bus as a challenger to the tram.

Manchester was not the only customer for Crossleys. In 1931 Bury Corporation took delivery of five diesel-engined Condors, with 48-seat rear-entrance front-exit bodies with two stairways. These were concentrated on one of Bury's routes which was claimed to be the first in the world to be entirely worked by diesel-engined buses. Rochdale was another buyer; the corporation's first buses in 1926 were Guy and Dennis single deckers, but in 1930 with the advent of the tram replacement scheme the double-decker made its debut, and then regular deliveries took place of Condors as well as single deck Alphas.

In the Manchester fleet the notable development of 1934 was the introduction of what was known as the 'Mancunian' double-decker, a vehicle which gave its distinctive look to the city's transport picture; put on the road between 1934 and 1936, more than 150 of them seemed to attain a remarkable degree of ubiquity and longevity. A corresponding single-deck version was also produced, still retaining the name of Alpha. The next milestone in styling came in 1936 with the 'streamline' design, a sort of cleaned-up version of the Mancunian; distinguished by rounded downward sloping corner windows, its most prominent feature was the livery which incorporated sweeping curved markings disappearing into infinity in an effect that matched contemporary super-cinema decor. Chassis were supplied by both Crossley and Leyland, while bodies originated from various sources. A corresponding single-deck version was also produced in the same art deco style, but still with the cut-away rear entrance that was much favoured at the time.

For the motorbus the 1930s proved to be the decade of the municipal double-decker. In Greater Manchester, as elsewhere, the bus arrived in the mainstream of urban transport. Hitherto it had generally taken a secondary role, filling in gaps in the tramway network, running along back streets, linking outlying communities away from the tracks, or making fast interurban connections. For such uses the conditions often dictated the single-decker; either the traffic was not heavy enough to justify the double-decker, or the route traversed narrow streets, sharp corners or awkward hills where only the single-decker could operate in safety. Often the municipal bus had had to compete with the speedy independent or 'pirate'.

By the end of the 1920s things were different. The double-decker had come of age; now fitted with

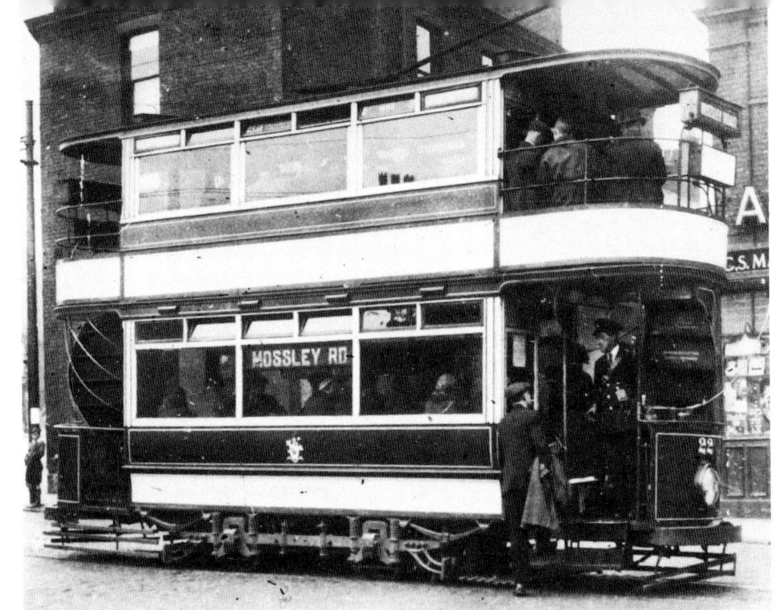

pneumatic tyres and covered top deck, it looked like the answer to the municipalities' nagging question 'What shall we do about the trams?' Now it could take over the heavily-trafficked routes on the wide main roads. Municipal bus fleets began to evolve from a handful of single-deckers on the byways to whole arrays of double-deckers on the principal highways.

The capacity of the double-decker was now enough to challenge the tram. It accommodated 48 to 52 passengers, comparable with the typical four-wheel car which had seats for between 52 and 58; this may still have been marginally less, but a good number of trams were of the open-balcony type where eight or ten of the passengers had to be seated on the open ends exposed to the weather, whereas the bus was not only all-enclosed but had upholstered seats.

But what about Manchester, where the big bogie double-deck trams had seats for 78 or 80 passengers? How could the 48-seat bus effectively replace such a vehicle? The answer lay in two facts of operational life. Just how often was the full capacity of the big tramcar needed? In peak hours perhaps it was crammed to overflowing, but this was only a brief period of time; for most of the day it ran with much less than a full load, so that excess capacity was being hauled needlessly around. The bus could therefore be quite an adequate substitute. And, then, in the peak the bus gained from its extra mobility; it could take a full load

Above: Invaluable in concentrated rush hours, the big bogie tramcar represented excess capacity at slack periods; two Manchester 80-seat cars pause for a quiet moment at suburban West Didsbury.   *W. A. Camwell*

into town with the minimum of delay without having to wait in a long line of cars tied to one set of tracks, and then could hurry back for more. It could operate short workings, it could integrate with other routes, and it was quicker in negotiating junctions; thus its mobility more than compensated for its lower nominal capacity. Its effective capacity proved to be higher.

But what about the weather? Supporters of the tram still claimed one trump card: the tram's ability to keep going in fog, a meteorological condition not entirely unknown in Manchester. Since they kept to their fixed tracks, the trams could maintain a service in the worst of foggy weather, while the 'mobile' motor bus was handicapped by its very mobility; it had to crawl along the kerb or just stay put in its garage if visibility did not permit it to see where it was going. Hence if Manchester scrapped its railed vehicles and relied entirely on the 'mobile' bus, said the tramcar adherents, it was likely to suffer a total transport shutdown when fog blanketed the city.

They had reckoned without the ingenuity of Stuart Pilcher. Not for nothing had he earned the title of 'the foremost advocate of omnibus substitution for tramways' and he was determined to prove that his buses could provide an all-weather capability at least equal to that of the older form of transport. Indeed,

with the growing dependence on the bus as the conversion process gathered momentum, it was crucial to the city's wellbeing that there should be no loss of reliability.

Accordingly an all-out attack was launched to overcome the fog menace. Corporation motorcars, together with vans enlisted from the parcels service, were prepared for action; they were embellished with powerful swivelling headlamps by which they could pick out the kerb ahead, while at the rear an impressive vertical string of lamps shone like a beacon for the benefit of the buses which would follow in their wake. At the onset of fog, these brightly-lit vehicles took up their patrol duties, their lights piercing the gloom as they revealed the way for the buses following them. Motorcycles and sidecars similarly equipped were also pressed into the good work. Kerbs were whitened and marked by hurricane lanterns, speedily distributed by van when fog threatened, while the various local authorities in the area also participated with liberal applications of whitewash and whole batteries of lamps along the roadside. As a final touch, conductors were issued with white dust costs, to be donned if they had to alight and guide their charges.

Such measures helped to keep the growing numbers of buses running through the winters of the 1930s. Pilcher was able to claim that the bus was just as capable as the tram of maintaining its mileage and revenue-earning ability during foggy weather, even if some passengers waiting at bus stops on gloomy nights might have voiced their scepticism.

5
Electric rails and roads

Manchester's electric railways

'A wealthy cotton spinner in Manchester leaves the Exchange and arrives at the Express Railway Station for his first experience of lightning travelling.'
Arthur H. Beavan, *Tube, Train, Tram and Car*, 1903

The first railway to be electrified in the Manchester area was not the most obvious candidate. North of Manchester, a $3\frac{3}{4}$ mile single line opened in 1882 ran from Bury to Holcombe Brook, serving in part some of the town's suburbs but for the rest still largely open country on the edge of the hills. Bury Corporation's electric trams later paralleled the railway as far as Tottington, and to meet the competition the LYR introduced one of its steam rail motors in 1905, also adding roadside halts where passengers could board and alight almost as on a tramway.

Electrification from Bury to Holcombe Brook was carried out in 1913 on the overhead system at 3,500V dc, the original rolling stock consisting of two motor cars and two trailers. The installation was of an experimental nature, under the auspices of the Dick, Kerr company, with the object of proving equipment for a possible South American order of some magnitude, and was not to set the pattern for the LYR's further electrification.

The first electric railway in Manchester itself was the adjoining Manchester-Bury line, on which the LYR inaugurated electric operation on 17 April 1916. This line not only connected the city with neighbouring Bury, but in between served flourishing residential suburbs such as Crumpsall, Heaton Park and Prestwich; situated on rising ground to the north of the city, these suburbs had grown in population by some 30% in the dozen or so years prior to electrification, and growth looked like continuing under the stimulus of improved train services. From the railway's point of view, these suburbs were sufficiently far removed from the centre of the city for the train to offer a useful time

Above: An unusual sight as the entire stock of the Holcombe Brook line coupled together makes a trial run. *GEC Traction*

Below left: One of the Bury-Holcombe Brook electric cars in its original condition, operating under the overhead wires with two pantographs. *GEC Traction*

advantage over parallel tram routes. Developments in the district included new housing schemes and the recent purchase by the city of Heaton Park as a recreation area. Already in 1912 the rail service had been substantially augmented, with as many as 20 additional trains a day, so the traffic clearly justified electric traction.

Work on electrification had started by 1914, but wartime conditions had slowed down the project, and as a result it was not possible to introduce a full service of electric trains immediately, the new trains being slotted into the schedule as they became available. In general they corresponded to the steam trains they replaced, but as more came in speeds were improved, with a reduction in journey time of some 25%. The timing of the steam trains from Manchester to Bury of 32min was reduced to 24min with the electrics while in the opposite direction (which was with the grade) the time of 29min was cut to 22min.

Instead of the overhead of the Holcombe Brook line, the new project used the third rail system operating at 1,200V dc; in view of the high voltage, side contact collector shoes were employed with a suitably protected live rail, while a fourth rail was situated between the running rails and bonded to them as the main medium for return current. The trains built by the LYR were notable in being of all-metal construction, and were believed to be the first such, not only in Britain but probably in the world. Cars were of the end-door saloon type, with a driving compartment at each end, so that the maximum flexibility of train formation was possible. The normal make-up was a five-car train, comprising three third class motor cars and two first/third trailers, giving a total seating capacity of 72 first class and 317 third class. The first class sections were upholstered in tapestry, while the thirds had more spartan rattan seating.

Despite their wartime initiation, the new trains functioned well. A correspondent to *The Railway Magazine* in the winter of 1916-17 reported that 'services continued to work very satisfactorily, the 20min service being still maintained'; it was not at all affected by the heavy frost, while 'even in the thickest fog, as a rule the trains arrived so little late that they were generally able to leave either terminus on time'.

Meanwhile, the Holcombe Brook line had been undergoing conversion to the third rail system in line with its longer neighbour, and operation was re-introduced on 29 March 1918 using the third-rail. In the obvious interests of safety, suitable platforms were built at the ground level halts where previously passengers had boarded or alighted by means of retractable steps on the cars.

Rumours abounded of the LYR's plans for more electrification; had it not produced a wonderful new electric locomotive which would haul main line expresses, and had this not been seen undergoing trials on the Holcombe Brook branch? But wartime str-

Right: The Holcombe Brook electric cars were originally fitted with retractable steps for use at the rail-level halts. *GEC Traction*

Below: A five-car train of the Manchester-Bury electric stock in Lancashire & Yorkshire days. Each train comprised three motor cars and two trailers, but each car was fitted with driving compartment to allow flexibility of make-up. Note the protected side-contact live rail and the return current rail, which was bonded to the running rails. *GEC Traction*

ingencies, followed by postwar control, the merger with the LNWR in 1922 and the subsequent grouping in 1923, stifled such visions. In 1924, though, the newly-formed LMS was considering electrification of lines from Manchester Victoria to Oldham and on to Shaw, together with the branch to Royton, involving about 12 miles of route. The work was to have included improvements at Oldham and Werneth, a new station at Shaw, and electrification of sidings at Newton Heath. Electrification of the Irk Valley loop would have enabled the services to have avoided the complicated junctions at Miles Platting. The third-rail system was to have been used, with side contact as on the Bury line, and the trains were also to have been of the centre corridor type. A basic 20min service would have operated to Shaw and Royton, with additional trains between Manchester and Oldham. At a later stage it was possible that electrification would be continued from Shaw to Rochdale, as well as over the line to Rochdale via Castleton, thus completing an out-and-back circuit from Manchester over lines which had traditionally carried a heavy local service.

Though all this was not to come to fruition, the Bury line continued to function. Traffic increased and

Left: Further electrification schemes were envisaged in the Manchester area, such as the lines to Oldham and Rochdale, but these did not materialise, and the faithful 2-4-2 tanks were left to do the work. LMS No 10621 was formerly LYR No 1008.
Ian Allan Library

Below: The Manchester South Junction & Altrincham Railway was paralleled by a tramway from 1907 and later by motorbuses. The clock tower marks Altrincham station as a Manchester tramcar passes in this view of about 1910. *R. Brook*

two new stations were opened: at Besses o' the Barn in 1933 and Bowker Vale in 1938. The original trains soldiered on until replaced by British Rail stock at the end of the 1950s. Holcombe Brook was not so fortunate; electric operation ended on 25 March 1951, when a steam train took over until 7 May 1952, after which the line was closed.

The next scheme that had materialised involved the Altrincham line. Electrification of the Manchester South Junction & Altrincham Railway had been proposed at least as early as 1911; an electric tramway had started running parallel to it in 1907. More severe competition had arisen with the advent of motorbus services during the 1920s, and in 1928 the joint owners of the railway (the LMS and the LNER) announced that electrification was to go ahead at a cost of about £500,000. The work was carried out by the LMS, using the overhead system operating at 1,500V dc; this was the first passenger line to adopt this standard, which had been recommended by the Railway Electrification Committee in its report in 1928 and proposed by the Weir Committee on main line electrification in 1931.

Electric services started on 11 May 1931. Two new

stations were opened to serve growing residential traffic and to cater for further traffic expected with the faster and better trains; Dane Road was situated between Stretford and Sale, and Navigation Road between Timperley and Altrincham. In addition, the old Cricket Ground station, hitherto open only on occasions of cricket and football matches, was now opened regularly and was renamed Warwick Road. In the first three years after electrification, receipts on the line rose by some 30%.

Rolling stock comprised 22 three-car sets built by Metropolitan-Cammell. These were of the compartment type, this design being adopted to permit of the fastest possible loading and unloading. Originally in the light green livery of the line, the trains comprised third class motor cars seating 72 passengers, com-

posite trailers with seats for 48 third and 40 first class passengers, and driving trailers to seat 108 third class passengers. Trains could thus be made up of three or six cars, with six being the normal. Seven-car trains were tried for a period in 1939, in order to cater for increased wartime traffic, and for this purpose a further eight trailers of different types were drafted in; however, this working did not prove satisfactory, since pulling up the longer trains within the confines of the platforms was no easy task under blackout conditions.

Again there were expected to be extensions at the time of the electrification of the Altrincham line. Ultimately it was envisaged that electric operation would be projected to form a loop continuing from London Road through Longsight, Mauldeth Road, and East Didsbury, and to Gatley, together with a

94

connection on to the CLC line through Northenden and Baguley to reach Altrincham. One thing at least was obvious: already the different systems of electrification were raising obstacles to any integrated route network.

The South Junction retained its nominal separate identity until nationalisation in 1948, when it became part of the London Midland Region of British Railways. In 1958 the Altrincham service was cut back to Oxford Road to allow the section from there to London Road to be taken over by the new 25kV system being installed on the Manchester-London main line. Then in 1959 the construction of a new Oxford Road station was started, including a new platform and extension of existing platforms to cater for longer trains, in readiness for its connection with the

service to and from Crewe, and eventually the Altrincham line was converted and linked to give through services on to the main line.

Back in 1926, an ambitious scheme of more than local significance was drawn up by the LNER for the electrification of the main line between Manchester and Sheffield, via the Woodhead Tunnel. The line carried a heavy goods traffic, especially coal across the Pennines from Yorkshire into industrial Lancashire, and was plagued with severe gradients, including a 20-mile climb up to the Woodhead Tunnel. However, the scheme was deferred; this was a time when the railways were not affluent enough to afford such costly capital projects, but in 1936 it was revived in a revised form backed by government financing. By 1939 the work was well under way with visible evidence in the shape of gantries for the 1,500V dc overhead equipment. Then of course came the war, and further work had to be postponed. Still, it was possible to construct one of the new locomotives, which in 1941 underwent trials on the Altrincham line.

The scheme was carried to completion after the war, and on 14 September 1954 electric operation was inaugurated between Manchester and Sheffield, together with local services at the Manchester end to Hadfield and Glossop. Worked by multiple-units on a faster and more frequent schedule than in steam days, these local services helped to build up regular residential traffic flows into these areas, even though the through passenger service later declined.

Another new phase came with the introduction of electric operation between Manchester and Crewe as part of the electrification of the main lines between Manchester and Liverpool and London. The first part, the Manchester-Crewe operation via the Wilmslow line, presaged the later introduction on 18 April 1966 of a new Manchester-London schedule of 2hrs 35min, compared with the former best steam time of 3hr 10min, all a far cry from the incredible $4\frac{1}{2}$ days of 200 years earlier.

Manchester might have had a high-speed electric railway much sooner if a plan of 1900 had reached fruition. In 1901 the Act for the 'Manchester & Liverpool Electric Express Railway' received the Royal Assent, and early in 1902 it was confidently expected that 'construction will be proceeded with at once'. This expectation proved more than optimistic. Had the scheme materialised, it would doubtless have proved to be one of the wonders of the transport world, for this

Right: How we might have travelled on the proposed 'Manchester and Liverpool Electric Express Railway' of 1901; the interior of a Behr monorail car with its 'comfortably upholstered' back-to-back seats.

Electric Express Railway was to have been a monorailway capable of speeds of 110mile/h, thus covering its 35-mile route in about 20min with no intermediate stops.

Based on the principles devised by the Belgian inventor F. B. Behr, the trains were to consist of single cars, each carrying about 40 passengers on 'comfortably upholstered' seats which would be 'separated and placed back to back in the middle'. The lighting would be 'excellent' and the ventilation 'perfect', though to prevent accidents the windows would be fixed and the doors automatically locked while the car was in motion. Each car would be powered by four 160hp motors, while Westinghouse brakes would enable it to stop from a speed of 110mile/h in about 800yd; the brakes would be aided by 'Mr Behr's ingenious device' consisting of louvres or shutters which could be opened to increase air resistance.

Cars would run every 10min, and it was envisaged that some 20,000 passengers a day would be carried. Safety would be ensured by an automatic signalling system, and by the fact that there would be no points or junctions on the line. However, later experience of high speed trains might frown on such features as the many curves ('all necessary in order to avoid conflict with the vested interests of other railway companies', as a contemporary account explained sadly) and the gradients as steep as 1 in 30 and even 1 in 25, which we are told would 'be of service in accelerating and braking the trains'. The Manchester terminus would have been at the west side of Deansgate, with the line departing via Salford, Pendleton and Eccles and continuing on through Warrington and Widnes to Liverpool

96

Perhaps anticipating the usual objections to high speed travel, Arthur H. Beavan in his *Tube, Train, Tram and Car* in 1903 gives us an answer:
'What useful purpose can be served by being able to get from Liverpool to Manchester in 20 minutes instead of over an hour? Do not existing railways bring merchant and broker, importer and manufacturer, face to face quickly enough, and are not telephones and telegraphs and the post sufficient to carry through big transactions between the centre of the cotton trade and the great city on the banks of the Mersey? Public opinion, which demands increasing speed in every phase of life, declares they are not sufficient; for we live in an impatient age'.

Impatient or not, neither manufacturer nor merchant, nor indeed anyone else, was destined to travel from Manchester to Liverpool by this high speed monorail. Though *The Railway Magazine* deplored the fact that there were people 'sanguine enough to speculate with the system' and to provide money to obtain the Act for a railway 'on this antique method', Beavan had seen the obvious difficulty: there were already three conventional railways, between them operating a frequent service carrying passengers between the two cities in 40 or 45min, and even a halving of the journey time only resulted in a saving of 20min. Yet it is interesting to note that many years later, in 1970, a study was under way for another high speed route between Manchester and Liverpool, this time using the newly developed hovertrain principle. But, like its predecessor, it was never built, and the conventional railway still performs, though it has still not been electrified.

The Underground that never was

'Manchester is at last to have its own tube railway.'
The Railway Magazine, 1912

One thing that Manchester had long hankered after but had never possessed was an underground railway. London had a whole network of them, Glasgow had one, and — perhaps most galling of all — even Liverpool had one, but somehow Manchester had missed out on this most prestigious of transport modes. Just why this should have been so was not entirely clear. Certainly it was not for the want of trying; proposals for an underground railway in the city had abounded since at least the start of this century.

In 1901, for example, when a 'tube boom' was honeycombing the London clay, 'a group of influential householders' in Manchester were seeking Parliamentary powers for the construction of a tube railway in their own city. The idea was to build a circular route which would connect the main railway stations: from Victoria to London Road, Oxford Road, Central, Exchange and back to Victoria. The cost was estimated at about £1.5million. Such a route had obvious merit in overcoming the long-felt disadvantage of the scattered railway stations; the north-south traveller faced a mile-long hike from Victoria and Exchange to London Road, while Central was little more central than the others. Passengers encumbered with luggage, and to whom time was money, were perpetually frustrated by the tedious interchange which necessitated a brisk walk through busy streets, a slow tram ride through the traffic of Market Street and Piccadilly, or a costly (and little faster) cab. Hence the idea of a north-south cross-city connection was a constant theme.

Although nothing materialised at this time, the basic idea was still alive in 1912. Again the plan was for a circle to link the main stations; from Victoria the line would go under High Street, where there would be a station at the junction with Market Street. Then it would continue under Piccadilly to London Road, where it would pass under Altrincham Street and Charles Street to Oxford Road station; here a triangular junction would be laid for a branch to Whitworth Park, serving the University. The circle would continue to Central, and then run beneath Deansgate to reach Victoria again. Altogether there would be eight stations.

The chances for the line seemed good; *The Railway Magazine* reported that, 'with the characteristic enterprise of the city, a considerable proportion of the necessary capital is already assured'. It pointed out that the underground would be 'of immense value in facilitating rapid transit in the city and its surroundings, and as a supplement to the extensive tramway services existing'. It went on to comment that, 'having an intimate acquaintance with the immense potentialities of the local traffic, we believe that the project will be a great success, and an advantage to all the trunk lines that serve Manchester'. Nevertheless, in spite of its apparent imminence, nothing came to pass, and soon World War 1 banished such thoughts.

After the war there were other obstacles, including the further upheaval caused by the Grouping of the railways, with the new Groups needing to put their own houses in order before they could consider becoming involved with new railways. Still, the idea was not allowed to rest, and by the middle of the 1920s Manchester City Council's Underground Railway Special Committee was considering a plan for an ambitious scheme covering not only the inner area but also the surrounding districts, extending into Salford and to Stretford and Prestwich. A system of some 14 miles was envisaged, at an estimated cost of around £4million. In 1926, while the committee's report was still awaited, there was talk of problems — not only engineering difficulties but, perhaps more ominous, financial concern.

Come 1928, however, and we were told that 'the scheme is going quietly and steadily forward', with a special committee on the point of putting a definite project to the city council. This turned out to be an even more ambitious scheme; it proposed as much as 35 miles of routes, which it was believed could be put into operation within eight years from the start of construction. There would be both an inner and an outer circle, linking with the main lines radiating from the city. Initially there could be just an inner circle, together with a line running out to the suburb of Withington, a distance of four miles; this part of the project would cost an estimated £5million and could be

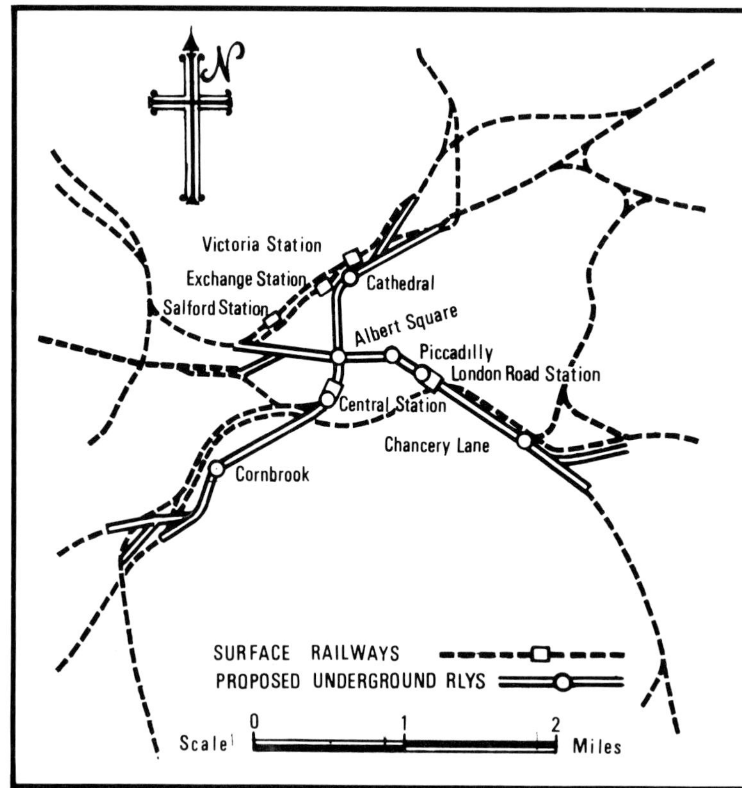

Left: Manchester's proposed underground railway of 1928, showing connections across the city centre and junctions with the main line railways to link with suburban services.

Below right: The proposed underground railway was intended to ease congestion in central Manchester by diverting traffic from the streets. The growing problem is exemplified in this 1930 view: a line of tramcars inches its way through the crowded city. *R. Brook*

expected to carry about 100 million passengers a year. The cost of the full scheme was put at a substantial £20million, and not surprisingly we were informed that 'the financial aspect of the proposals is receiving close consideration'. No doubt this 'close consideration' encouraged the presentation later in the same year of a more modest project by Henry Mattinson, General Manager of the city tramways department.

Mattinson's scheme was for two lengths of underground railway beneath the main streets of the city, meeting at a central point where there would be an interchange station. These two sections would link up with existing surface lines, and would thus be able to give through cross-city services on suburban routes from all directions. The two underground routes would have comprised one from a junction near Old Trafford to a point near Collyhurst, and the other from near Ordsell Sidings in Salford to a location near Ardwick; both lines would have connected at each end with suburban lines which would have been electrified to enable cross-city services to be run. The underground sections would have totalled about seven miles in all, and would have met at a new central station near the Town Hall. It was suggested that their construction should be undertaken by the corporation, which would then lease them to the railway companies to operate. In association with the new system, the tram and bus services would have been modified in order to coordinate their operations with those of the railways.

This new system, Mattinson claimed, would 'afford to Manchester and the adjacent communities an almost limitless field of expansion for rapid transit facilities, which, supplemented by our tramway and omnibus system for shorter journeys, will give the community unrivalled local passenger transportation on a basis that gives every prospect of being financially sound'. He explained that the underground sections would serve to link up nine suburban routes on which 27 services were operating. The suburban rail lines into Manchester were conveying daily an average of 200,000 people into and out of the city's four main stations, and this traffic was sufficient to ensure an adequate return on the investment that would be required.

While it was agreed that Manchester had a valuable asset in its splendid network of railways, they did not in fact constitute a system since there was no co-ordination of services, each line being operated as a separate entity. Moreover, there was as yet only one electrified line (Manchester-Bury-Holcombe Brook) and there was an obvious need for further electrification in order to secure that the railways could offer the most attractive service. It was believed that if the new scheme was adopted, 'there would thus be created for the city a unified passenger transport system unique in the world'.

Again nothing came of it. There was the perennial problem of cost, of course, but there was also the thorny problem of co-ordination. Such a scheme not only called for the co-operation of the railways in the planning and working of the proposed lines, but also required the concomitant electrification which formed an essential element of the proposed cross-city underground working. Although it was anticipated that the Government would have given financial assistance as a measure of unemployment relief, the railway companies were not in a position to undertake the large-scale electrification proposed in the full scheme. The question of an integrated transport system was not to be resolved for a long time yet, but the need for such co-ordinated planning was one of the strongest arguments put forward in the protracted discussions for an area transport board. Meanwhile, following the death of Mattinson, Manchester had a new Transport Manager and had already begun to go deeply into the bus business for suburban operations.

A connection between the main railway stations continued to be seen as a desirable objective, and the SELNEC plan of the 1960s envisaged the 'Picc-Vie' line between the renamed London Road and Victoria to connect railways north and south of the city; it was expected to be in operation by 1978, though there were no signs of it by the start of the 1980s. Such a link was also in view as part of a rapid transit system incorporating suburban railways on new rights of way. In 1964, the Manchester transport manager, A. F. Neal, presented a report to the city council urging examination of the possible introduction of a rapid transit system; it suggested that there should be particular emphasis on the development of express bus services on reserved lanes along the city's main traffic arteries.

In 1966, when the idea was still in the air, *Passenger Transport* commented that Manchester's buses were 'gradually being bogged down by increasing traffic congestion as more and more private cars come into use'. To solve the problem considerable thought had been given to such possibilities as a monorail rapid transit system, for which a preliminary estimate for a 16-mile route put the cost at over £20 million. Such a cost, said *Passenger Transport*, 'could only be justified on the grounds that the system would be adequate for many years ahead and that there is no better alternative'.

The 'better alternative' was agreed to be the well-tried 'duorail' (as the vogue word of the time had it) but again this was baulked by the high capital cost. The time never seems right to justify the investment in transport assets, and Manchester's plans remained 'the Underground that never was'.

The mixed fortunes of the trolleybus

'Trackless trolley cars have undergone considerable improvement, and there are circumstances which may warrant their introduction.'

J. M. McElroy, General Manager,
Manchester Corporation Tramways, 1914

Unlike the tramcar, the trolleybus never really flourished on Lancashire soil. There were exceptions; Manchester's system grew into one of the largest in Britain, almost in spite of itself, while the long-lived interurban vehicles of the South Lancashire Transport Company became something of an institution. Among pioneering efforts, early installations were set up at Ramsbottom, Stockport and Wigan, but these did not develop into fully-fledged systems. Somehow the trolley vehicle rarely seemed to arouse great enthusiasm. If we seek the reasons for this, we might find a clue in the firmly established network of municipal tramway services, while for other routes the motorbus offered the advantage of flexibility, as it did when the time came to consider replacing the trams. So, while the area's tramcars in their heyday num-

bered over 2,000, the trolleybuses never exceeded a total of more than about 300.

First in the field was Stockport Corporation, which put trolley vehicles into service on 10 March 1913 on a route less than two miles long, from the town centre in St Peter's Square to the borough boundary at Offerton. Though modest in extent, the installation was notable in being the only one in Britain to make use of the Bremen or Lloyd-Kohler method of current collection; this involved a flexible trolley running on two wires mounted one above the other. There was only a single set of wires along the route, so when two cars running in opposite directions met, their respective trolleys were simply unhooked and exchanged. Another unorthodox feature was that lattice standards were used to support the wires. Supplied by Daimler with Brush single deck bodies, the three vehicles were also unusual for the period in have foot-operated controllers, as against the normal contemporary hand-operated controller as on a tramcar.

The whole installation had cost an estimated total of £8,000 (including £4,000 for road works) compared with the sum of £14,000 that would have been

required for the construction of a single-track tramway. It had originally been intended that the trolleybus route should be continued on to Marple, but the neighbouring local authority at Hazel Grove proved unwilling to accept the new vehicles over its roads. Operation continued reasonably well for a time, but World War 1 cut off the source of spares in Germany, so that maintenance became a problem; regular services petered out by about 1919, although occasional journeys ran until 1920.

In Ramsbottom, the local authority toyed for a long time with the idea of installing tramways, just like any other self-respecting up-to-date town, but eventually it decided that the new trackless trams would be a cheaper proposition; and, after all, if they proved to be successful, then they could be replaced by real trams.

Accordingly Ramsbottom closely followed Stockport by opening its installation in the same year of 1913, its one route extending from Edenfield to Holcombe Brook station. It worked moderately well for several years, employing three Railless Electric Traction single-deckers using the Schiemann method of current collection, but it finally succumbed in 1931 when motorbuses took over.

Meanwhile Wigan Corporation had also introduced the new mode of transport, when on 7 May 1925 trolley vehicles began operation on the town's Martland Mill route, the first in the area where trolleybuses replaced trams. The decision was perhaps not surprising; Wigan had long been plagued with problems such as tramways on two different gauges, running on tracks affected by subsidence due to mining. The problem of gauge had almost been solved, with most of the narrow gauge track having been relaid to standard. While there was not much that could be done about subsidence, the removal of tram tracks minimised the chance of this phenomenon disrupting the flow of traffic. However, one narrow gauge route remained; what was to be done with it?

Conversion of gauge had been a costly business and, as it proved, was to become a major capital burden on the undertaking. So on this final route a cheaper solution was sought. Investigation revealed four possibilities. The tramway could be reconstructed to standard gauge at a cost of £35,758, or part of the tramway could be rebuilt with the rest replaced by buses, at a cost of only £26,122. Or the whole service could be replaced by motorbuses, involving the

Below left: 'Stockport Corporation's trolley omnibus service is the first in this country equipped with a flexible trolley connection . . . One pair of wires is sufficient for vehicles travelling in either direction, the current collector gear being unhooked and exchanged by drivers coming in opposite directions, at any convenient meeting place' (*Tramway and Railway World,* 1913).

Below: End of the road for Stockport's trolleybuses: Nos 2 and 3 stand forlornly in the depot after the cessation of service in 1920.   *C. Carter*

purchase of four single-deckers at a cost of £6,120. The fourth possibility was the reconstruction of the route for trolley vehicle operation, for which the cost would be £8,305.

Although not the cheapest alternative, the trolleybus option was chosen, in view of the existence of electrical supply equipment already in use for the tramways, as well as the potential for more economical working. Operation began with a fleet of four Brush-bodied Straker Clough single-deckers. This proved to be the extent of the town's trolley venture, and the end of tramway operation in 1931 meant that the maintenance of a mere four electric vehicles on one short route was just not worth while.

In Wigan, as in several others of the earlier trolleybus installations, the obstacle was that the trolley vehicles comprised only a small element in a total transport undertaking devoted to tramways (and later to the motorbus) while the use of non-standard equipment quickly made them obsolescent at a time when trolleybus design was advancing rapidly. It was also their misfortune that they could usually only be 'second best'; the busy routes along the good roads were already dominated by the trams, leaving the trolleybus to bump along the badly-made byways.

Very soon after Wigan had started, two more local authorities entered the field. Ashton and Oldham installed a joint route between the two towns in place of trams, to provide the first example of jointly-worked interurban trolleybus operation. Ashton had been considering the possibility of the new mode of transport

Above: Ashton Railless single-deck trolleybus No 51 is smartly turned-out in this late 1920s view, although the solid tyres gave a hard ride over the old tram tracks. *C. Carter*

The evolution of the trolleybus: two examples from Ashton. *Above right:* No 51, one of the Short-bodied Railless vehicles of 1925, manoeuvres outside the depot.

Right: A 1940 Crossley, with characteristic curvaceous bodywork, enters Manchester on the joint service, past an array of poster hoardings advertising the famous Belle Vue Gardens as well as the Opera House and the Deansgate cinema. *Both: C. Carter*
129, 130

for some time, for use on its route to Hathershaw at the boundary with neighbouring Oldham, since the existing tram tracks were badly in need of renewal. Then in 1924 Oldham decided to come in with its neighbour and become a trolleybus operator. The benefit was obvious; if Ashton went ahead alone, the through tram service between the two towns would be disrupted, with the likely result that dissatisfied customers would desert to private buses which did not have regard to frontiers. To continue the service it was necessary to adopt the type of vehicle that Ashton had decided on, so Oldham got its own powers to operate trolley vehicles in order to take its share in the joint operation.

Service was inaugurated on 12 August 1925, employing eight Railless single-deckers, six belonging

to Ashton and two to Oldham, and it was not long before it was reported that the new vehicles were 'giving great satisfaction to passengers'. However, this pleasant state of affairs proved to be shortlived: vibration of the vehicles along the setts disturbed local residents, while working costs appeared disappointingly high. Oldham became disillusioned, and little more than a year later it withdrew from the partnership, put its trams back, and terminated its brief career as a trolleybus operator. Ashton was more persistent, continuing to run its own trolley vehicles as far as the boundary, and eventually entering into another partnership, this time with Manchester, with whom its relationship turned out to be more enduring.

Most ambitious and most distinctive of the trolleybus undertakings within the area was that of the South Lancashire Transport Company. No doubt such characteristics had been inherited from tramway days when the company had visions of an extensive network of routes, most of which were destined never to see the light of day. Now under the South Lancashire Transport Act of 1929 the company obtained powers to replace its tramways by trolleybuses, changing the appropriate part of its name from 'Tramways' to 'Transport' at the same time.

The first conversion took place in 1930 when trolleybuses were installed on the route from Atherton to Ashton-in-Makerfield, being extended to St Helens in 1933. Also in 1931 conversion took place on the lengthy and roundabout Atherton-Farnworth route, followed in 1933 by the route from Leigh through Atherton to Bolton. This last move brought trolleybuses into Bolton for the first time, although Bolton continued to work its own trams as far as its boundary at Four Lane Ends. This situation continued until 1936 when Bolton Corporation itself became a trolleybus owner, with the purchase of four vehicles for the purpose of working this part of the route within its boundaries. As it happened, Bolton must have been one of the most self-effacing trolleybus operators of all time, for its vehicles were indisguishable from those of the SLT fleet and were housed in the SLT's depot. Bolton had thought long and deep about converting its tramway system to trolleybuses, and it continued to have such thoughts from time to time over the years to come, but somehow it never got round to owning more than these four somewhat anonymous vehicles.

Like the tramways before it, the SLT's trolley system exuded a sense of frustration. True, some of its vehicles did go somewhere; the joint route into St Helens, for example, or the workings into Bolton. But

The character of the South Lancashire company's trolleybus undertaking is well captured in these two views:
Right: The industrial background provides a setting for this Roe-bodied Guy six-wheeler as it reverses at Mosley Common, while:
Below: A rebuilt Guy four-wheeler negotiates narrow streets in Atherton on its way to Leigh. *R. Brook*

what could one make of a 14-mile route (strong contender for being the longest in the country) where the two termini were no more than five miles apart as the crow flies. Such was the case with the Atherton-Farnworth route, which pursued a roundabout circuit through Swinton and Worsley, coming into Salford territory and approaching Manchester, and ending up not far from Bolton, but never actually succeeding in reaching any of these places. Then in the other direction, when it seemed all set towards Wigan, it veered off again and went to St Helens instead. Such topographical quirks were of course an inheritance from tramway days when so many of the plans never materialised; had they done so in later days, there could have been through trolleybuses from Manchester and Salford to Bolton, Wigan and St Helens, and possibly even to Liverpool.

Even as it stood, the SLT route-mileage reached the respectable total of some 30 miles. Yet to work this extensive mileage there were only about 70 vehicles, a reflection of the fact that the headways on some routes were wider than might have been the case on a more compact purely urban undertaking. Its territory included a number of mining villages, and there were even glimpses of the open country in the vicinity of Worsley. An odd piece of layout was the short length of 'reserved track', a legacy of tramway days, where the trolleybuses jolted over a piece of unmade road behind a row of houses.

The gift of eternal youth seemed to have been bestowed on the SLT's vehicles. Thirty years of faithful service sat very lightly upon them; true, some had been given a species of face lift with new front ends, but basically many early comers retained their original form. The first vehicles were six-wheel Guys with Roe lowbridge bodies, since restrictive bridges afflicted nearly all routes. The four Bolton vehicles were Leylands with Roe highbridge bodies, while the only postwar additions to the SLT fleet were Weymann-bodied Sunbeams. Contraction of trolley operation got under way in 1956 when the Bolton short workings were withdrawn, thus ending that town's career as trolleybus owner, and then the rest of the SLT system ceased in 1958.

In Manchester, the idea of trolleybuses was not a new one, although it took a long time to gain acceptance. As early as 1908 a deputation from the city's tramways committee had been to the Continent to examine trolley installations there and had returned sufficiently impressed to recommend that a suitable clause to give the city powers to operate such vehicles should be inserted in the corporation's Bill the following year. Although this was done, Manchester had to wait many more years yet before it was to see trolleybuses in its streets.

When it came, the decision did not appear to emanate from either enthusiasm or unanimity. In 1935 the Transport Committee had proposed the replacement of the Ashton Old Road group of tram routes by motorbuses, but this proposal had been rejected by the city council, which instead stipulated that the trams should be retained until they could be replaced by trolleybuses. Although the committee continued to prefer the motorbus, in 1936 the council decided that the replacement should be by trolleybus, and the necessary powers were obtained in conjunction with the Corporation of Ashton, which would be involved in the changeover as partner on the routes concerned.

Estimated to cost £112,306, the conversion covered the introduction of 43 vehicles working on $6\frac{1}{2}$ miles of route. 20 56-seat four-wheelers would be obtained at £2,200 each and 23 68-seat six-wheelers at £2,600 each, in order to determine which size was best suited to the needs of Manchester's traffic. Accordingly, contracts were placed with Crossley for 12 six-wheel and 10 four-wheel chassis, and with Leyland for 11 six-wheel and 10 four-wheel chassis, the bodies for all 43 vehicles to be supplied by Crossley, with electrical equipment by Metropolitan-Vickers.

Crossley's association with the new fleet kept the orders in the home town. Crossley had produced its first trolleybus in 1936, a 68-seat six-wheeler with Metropolitan-Cammell Weymann body, and this had undergone trials in Ashton before entering service with that operator. Later in the same year the firm produced its first four-wheel trolleybus, which again underwent tests in Ashton. The same town's wires also served as the proving ground in 1937 for one of Manchester's first trolleybuses before the city's own system was ready to receive it.

A change of plan came before operations started, since Manchester City Council decided that the Ashton New Road tram services should also be replaced, following the recommendation of the transport committee in view of the close relationship between the two groups of routes. This addition to the scheme called for a further 33 vehicles, of which 18 were to be four-wheelers and 15 six-wheelers, thus bringing the total intended fleet to 76. The vehicles were designed to attain a maximum speed of 36mile/h, and to maintain a scheduled speed of 11mile/h on the basis of eight stops of five seconds each per mile

Inauguration took place on 10 March 1938, with the introduction of trolley vehicles on both Ashton Old Road and Ashton New Road, while at the same time a new depot was opened in Rochdale Road. The Old Road route continued through Ashton and on to Stalybridge, making a jointly-worked route of about nine miles. The SHMD had obtained powers to operate trolleybuses in 1936, but in fact it did not participate in operations. At the Manchester end of the system, a new one-way loop was brought into use to facilitate working in the congested area and to provide a suitable central terminal. The loop, about a mile and a quarter round, proceeded inward by way of Fairfield Street and Portland Street into Piccadilly and then into London Road.

Those who supported electric traction, and were reluctant to see the trams go on this score, were gratified to learn that the trolleybuses required more energy per mile than the tramcars, so that the load on the city's Electricity Department would not merely be retained but would be increased. But any prospect of wholesale replacement was soon dashed, and the trolley vehicles were basically to be confined to a few routes on one side of the city, with no cross-city connections. Nevertheless, at its maximum the system extended over a route mileage of 44, including 17 miles which were beyond the city boundaries in the areas of Ashton and the SHMD. The last of the routes survived until 1966, when trolleybus operation by both Manchester and Ashton came to an end.

Right: The Manchester trolleybus: typical of the prewar fleet when both four-wheelers and six-wheelers were evaluated. Here No 1081, a six-wheel Crossley-bodied Leyland of 1938 has already lost part of its streamlined livery, while four-wheeler 1941 Crossley No 1141 still sports its full array of curves. *C. Carter*

106

6
New dimensions

Manchester's Ship Canal

'The commerce of the world has been brought into direct communication by sea with your great city and its neighbourhood.'

Queen Victoria, 1894

Manchester's yearning for the sea proved to be a perennial stimulant to transport development, as witness the 18th century canals and the Liverpool & Manchester Railway. So it is not surprising that proposals were put forward with the object of making Manchester, some 35 miles from the coast, into a seaport. Many hard-headed folk condemned the idea as absurd, and for a long time it seemed that they might be right; only the doggedness of the promoters, plus the injection of substantial capital by the city itself, enabled the scheme to become a reality. Work on what critics derided as 'Manchester's Ditch' started in 1887, and such was the cost of construction that in 1890 Manchester Corporation was obliged to advance a sum of £5 million to ensure the completion of the project. The Manchester Ship Canal, from the Mersey estuary at Eastham to the Manchester Docks at Mode Wheel (actually in Salford) was opened for traffic on 1 Janary 1894, followed by an appropriate ceremonial inauguration by Queen Victoria on 21 May of the same year.

The coming of the Ship Canal had a widespread effect on the development of the Manchester area, and it is worth quoting the words of the canal's chief engineer, W. H. Hunter, writing 10 years after the opening:

'The Manchester Ship Canal has directly or indirectly affected beneficially the whole of the greatest industrial district on the face of the earth, while in the more limited area of which the city of Manchester is the heart and centre, many industries have been saved from extinction, and many others from decline and ultimate decay'.

In the years before the canal was built, Hunter continues:

'It was only too apparent that in Manchester and its environment of manufacturing towns decadence was stamped upon almost every industry, and that all progress was arrested. One manufacturer after another moved his works to the seaboard, leaving disused factories, empty warehouses, and uninhabited dwellings. . . Now, not only has decline been arrested and decay averted, but lines of new and vigorous growth have shot, and are shooting, out on every side. Expansion is universal. The change is definite and impressive,

Left: The port of Manchester: this general view of Nos 8, 7 and 6 docks taken in 1933 gives a good impression of the extent of the installations.
Manchester Ship Canal Company

Above: A busy scene at Manchester's No 9 dock in 1938. This dock was put out of use in 1940 owing to enemy action. *Manchester Ship Canal Company*

and has been due solely to the effect and influence of the Canal'.

Though later authorities might contend that Hunter somewhat overstated his case, there was no doubt that the advent of the canal had a crucial influence on the development of the economy of the area by providing direct access to the sea and hence cheaper transport for many commodities. For the first years there was a fight to obtain traffic; not unnaturally dock owners and shippers in Liverpool were not happy to see ships steaming past them to and from Manchester, while the railway companies also saw business being taken away. Nevertheless traffic on the ship canal built up: from less than a million tons in the first year, it rose to 3 million tons by 1900 and to more than 5 million tons in 1907. By this time the Manchester dock area covered some 400 acres, including a water space of more than a hundred acres, while there were eight docks with quays totalling more than six miles.

The Manchester docks were connected with the city's railways, so that the terminal was transformed into what a 1909 description terms 'a prodigious waterside railway goods depot'. The dock lines and sidings exceeded a length in total of 80 miles, forming a busy railway system in themselves. The railways came into being at the same time as the canal, and their first equipment consisted of material taken over from the contractors who had built the canal, but these had been replaced by the turn of the century when

Above: The Manchester Ship Canal Company employed its own fleet of steam locomotives to work its railways; typical of them is this 0-6-0 tank hauling a lengthy train of open wagons.   *Manchester Ship Canal Company*

there were 33 locomotives; by 1914 the Ship Canal Company's railways had a stock of some 60 locomotives, and by 1933 more than 70.

At the opening, the railway system amounted to only 14 route-miles, although the actual track-mileage was as much as 95. By 1903 this had increased to 35 route-miles, divided into several distinct units, the largest being at the Manchester terminal dock area, where connections were made with the main line companies. The growth of traffic on the ship canal company's lines is shown by the fact that, while in the first year of the canal's existence they carried only about 400,000 tons, by the first year of the new century this had risen to more than $1\frac{1}{2}$ million tons.

The canal was not nationalised when the other inland waterways of Britain were brought under state ownership by the Transport Act of 1947, and so the railways also remained under the Manchester Ship Canal Company to form the largest privately owned railway system in Britain. The track-mileage then amounted to some 200 and the motive power to nearly 70 locomotives, while more than 2,500 wagons were employed on internal traffic. Typical motive power comprised 0-6-0 tanks, most of which had flangeless centre wheels in order to negotiate the sharp curves, while the nature of their locale and traffic meant that all were fitted with spark arresters in the smokebox. The three connections with the main line railways in Manchester (at New Barnes, Bridgewater and Weaste) involved gradients as severe as 1 in 40, while the company also worked the lines of the Trafford Park Company, to which it was connected by a swing bridge across the Bridgewater Canal.

Steam traction continued dominant until 1959, when the first diesel locomotive was introduced by the company, and diesels eventually replaced all the steam power. By this time the port of Manchester effectively extended as far down from the city as the Queen Elizabeth oil dock at Eastham, opened in 1954, in which year the total traffic carried on the ship canal exceeded 16 million tons.

110

'The Park'

'Trafford Park is a modern miracle ... Yesterday the country seat of an aristocrat, today the rowdy seat of commerce.'

Walter Greenwood, *Love on the Dole*, 1933

A country estate of some 1,200 acres with a history traceable back to Domesday Book was to become one of the industrial successes of the Greater Manchester region, affecting the pattern of both industry and transport. Trafford Park was already on the banks of the Bridgewater Canal, but it was the coming of the Manchester Ship Canal that opened up its potential. The ship canal ran round one border of the estate, which was thus ideally situated for transformation into an adjunct of the great new port.

The Trafford Park Estates company was formed in 1896, two years after the opening of the ship canal, and as well as stimulating the pleasure aspect of the park with such amenities as a lake and a golf course, the company had in mind the creation of an industrial complex. This eventually grew into an area comprising some 200 industrial plants providing employment for about 50,000 people, together with ancillary services, among the major concerns being the electrical equipment manufacturer, British Westinghouse (later Metropolitan-Vickers). The park possessed its own railway network, amounting to more than 40 miles of tracks and giving access to the ship canal docks and the main line railways, together with private sidings into the principal industrial premises. While the Trafford Park company had locomotives of its own, the Manchester Ship Canal Company worked its own locomotives to connect with the docks, hauling loads over the swing bridge to mingle with the road traffic making its way along the streets of the estate.

Passenger transport services at different times saw Trafford Park with a mixture of varied modes of trac-

Below: There is little to suggest the rural antecedents of Trafford Park in this view of Third Avenue in 1938, as Salford tram No 159 and Manchester No 800 prepare for the evening rush hour. *W. A. Camwell*

tion, from a tramway with gas-powered cars to a steam train, and then to electric tramways that operated what was in effect a large loop around the estate, with a succession of cars in rush hours. The lines were taken over in 1905 by Manchester and Salford Corporations, who linked the services with their own networks to provide a complex of routes to cater for the needs of the workers. Bus services were taken over in 1925 by Lancashire United and extended over a wide district to the south and west.

A prophetic view of the significance of 'The Park' was expressed by a contributor to *The Railway Magazine* in 1903. Noting the potential of electric power in enabling factories to be established in outlying districts where land and rates were cheaper, he went on:

'The example of the British Westinghouse Company in establishing their works well outside Manchester, at Trafford Park, and of raising up a small township for their employees round the works, cannot fail to be extensively followed, more especially in those districts linked up by inter-urban electric tramway lines, with facilities for establishing a practical freight traffic. Thus will a substantial portion of the passenger traffic in cities be diverted into rural districts — and where then will be the prosperity of the municipal urban tramway lines?'

Although it did not work out quite like this (freight traffic on interurban tramways did not develop), Trafford Park was significant in representing a redistribution of industry and hence a change in transport needs. Not only did it provide a diversification of employment away from the area's traditional textiles, which were to suffer severely after 1914, but it created a new industrial centre which required a new set of transport services. The description of the locale as being 'well outside Manchester' now appears to belong to a different age, but the location of the park helped to shift the centre of gravity of the transport network. New services had to be supplied to connect the estate with a widespread suburban catchment area away from the established urban concentration, creating cross-suburban traffic flows beyond the confines of the tram routes.

Below: Both the industrialisation of Trafford Park and the establishment of the Manchester Ship Canal brought new traffic flows. Here Salford trams 205 and 209 await their loads at the Docks terminus in 1939.
W. A. Camwell

Manchester in the air

'The Daily Mail hereby undertake to pay the sum of £10,000 to the first person who flies in one day from London to Manchester.'

Daily Mail, 17 November 1906

Manchester's interest in the novelty of aerial travel might be said to have received its first inspiration from the landing of an intrepid aviator in a field at Didsbury in 1910. On 28 April of that year the Frenchman Louis Paulhan flew by aeroplane from London to Manchester to become the winner in a competition with a prize of £10,000 for the first person to make such a flight. Guided by the railway lines of the LNWR, which provided a special train to accompany him along the way, after many alarms and adventures Paulhan covered the last 24 miles in what was reported as the remarkable time of only 24 minutes. He came down at about 5.30 in the morning in Didsbury, where thousands of spectators were awaiting him.

The years of World War 1 stimulated the development of aviation, ready for its adaptation to civil purposes after the return of peace. In the summer of 1919 Manchester became the terminus of what has been claimed as the first regular air service to operate in England, when from May to September A. V. Roe

Below: Manchester's Barton aerodrome in 1932: all but one of the aircraft visible are biplanes, while the lines of spectators and the tents recall an era when air travel was still a novelty.
City of Manchester Local History Library

flew between Manchester, Southport and Blackpool, using a three-seater plane. A rail strike was on at the time, so perhaps a few frustrated passengers were encouraged to take to the air, though the low capacity of the service could hardly have proved an effective substitute for the usual trains; nor could the fare have made it available to more than an affluent minority: £4 4s single for a trip of less than 50 miles worked out at about 1s 8d a mile (8p).

In 1922 another pioneer operator, Daimler Airway, started a Manchester-London service to provide a connection with its London-Paris flights, and this is claimed as the first sustained internal English air route to London. It continued until 1924, employing a six-passenger DH4 biplane with a speed of 95mile/h. Operating cost at 1s 6d (7$\frac{1}{2}$p) per seat-mile still restricted air travel to the favoured few.

Although air transport made great advances during the 1920s with the growth of international and Empire air routes, internal services within Britain were still generally spasmodic and uneconomic. One reason was the lack of suitable aerodromes, and in 1928 the Air Ministry sent a circular letter to major cities and towns throughout the country, urging that steps should be taken towards the establishment of municipal aerodromes, which it believed would sooner or later be an essential part of all go-ahead municipalities. It called for prompt action in order to get the work under way before all the most suitable sites were occupied for other purposes or became prohibitively expensive. Manchester responded with alacrity, and already in that same year the city council agreed that it should 'reserve and acquire a site in or near Manchester for the purposes of an aerodrome'. In 1929 it set up an aerodrome special committee for this purpose.

So eager were the authorities to get on with the job that a temporary aerodrome was opened in 1929 at Wythenshawe, to become the first civic airport in Britain. At the opening, a noted aviator Capt A. K. Kingwill, broke his journey by air from London to Glasgow in order to give joy rides to members of the aerodrome committee so that they could have some taste of the pleasures to be derived from this new dimension in travel.

Meanwhile the more permanent aerodrome was under construction on land aleady owned by the

Right: Traffic at Manchester's Ringway airport increased rapidly in the postwar years; here passengers embark on a British European Airways' Trident, one of the larger aircraft serving Ringway in this period. *British Airways*

corporation at Barton, on Chat Moss, about six miles from the centre of the city and on the main road to Liverpool. This was accordingly opened in 1930. In anticipation, a newly formed company, Manchester Air Lines, which had already been operating from the temporary aerodrome, had been granted provisional permission to fly from Barton. The company had been established to operate local air services, as well as to convey passengers to London's Croydon airport where they could change to Continental services. It was also expected that during the holiday season there would be flights to such resort areas as the Isle of Man and the Lake District; it was hoped that the cost would be kept as low as 1s (5p) a mile, which would make air travel as cheap as taking a taxi.

With the increasing size and speed of aircraft during the 1930s, Barton was soon found to be inadequate for its purpose, and so a search was made for a site where a larger aerodrome could be established capable of

handling the growing load. Hence in 1935 the city council received Air Ministry sanction for the construction to start at Ringway, some seven miles to the south of the city and not very far away from the original temporary site at Wythenshawe. The initial scheme for Ringway was estimated to cost about £180,000, and, with an area of some 600 acres of land available, it was envisaged that expansion would be possible to meet foreseeable future needs. Ringway was officially opened by the Secretary of State for Air on 25 June 1938.

During World War 2 Ringway was requisitioned by the Government and used by the RAF, and it was not until 1946 that civilian air services were resumed, the first international flight being made by Air France. Under the Civil Aviation Act of 1946, the Ministry of Aviation sought to take over Ringway, but the city council disputed this and eventually in 1953 agreement was reached for the airport to remain under municipal ownership and operation. The postwar years saw a great increase in the number of passengers handled at Ringway; from not much more than 30,000 in 1947, the number rose to a quarter of a million in 1954, and to over a million in 1962. By 1977 the total had increased to 3 million, and Ringway stood as the largest municipal airport in Britain.

Below: To operate its Ringway Airport services during the 1950s, Manchester Corporation used Burlingham-bodied Leyland Royal Tigers. The rear section of the unusual body had a raised saloon above the luggage compartment.
H. V. Burlingham, courtesy Ian Allan Library

7
Motorbus triumphant

Manchester decides

'The word "car" means omnibus or trolley bus.'
Manchester Corporation Passenger
Regulations 1950

Decisive defeat in Manchester for the cause of the electric vehicle, both tram and trolleybus, came in 1938 with a transport department report recommending replacement of all the city's remaining tramways within three years. The tramways still comprised some 45% of the transport undertaking, but the report urged that they should be superseded at as rapid a rate as possible, subject only to the supply of new buses and the retraining of the crews. The arguments against the tram were already well known and were not much elaborated on; compared with either motorbus or trolleybus, it was less profitable, slower and less mobile, and it contributed to traffic congestion, as well as being less suitable for through operation between one authority and another. The cost of the conversion was put at £875,820, based on the replacement of the surviving trams by 337 new motorbuses and 91 trolleybuses.

While it was accepted almost as a foregone conclusion that the trams should go, the interest of the report centres especially on the comparison between the respective merits of bus and trolleybus as a replacement. The trolleybus did not come out of it well. Perhaps this was a somewhat surprising verdict in view of the general widespread enthusiasm for this type of vehicle in Britain at this period; London, for example, was going in for the wholesale substitution of trolleybuses for trams, and its fleet was already the biggest in the country, while many other cities and towns throughout the land were opting for the trolleybus as the natural successor to the tram. Manchester reached a different conclusion.

The main charge against the trolleybus was its lack of mobility. Indeed we are led to conclude that in this respect it was little better than the tram; confined to its wires, the trolleybus was unable to be diverted to other routes if the need arose, it had to go slowly at junctions and round corners, one vehicle was unable to overtake another on the same route, and the overhead equipment disfigured the streets. Admittedly the trolleybus caused less obstruction than the tram, since it was able to deviate from its course to mingle with

Left: The merit of flexibility was urged for the motorbus; here an inbound Manchester tram has to wait while an SHMD Board short-working car reverses at Crown Point, Denton, before returning to Hyde. Motorcars parked at each side of the road do not aid traffic flow.
W. A. Camwell

Above right: While the advantages of the trolleybus were finely balanced, Manchester made the change on a few routes; tram 220 halts at Audenshaw (Snipe) on a 26B short working on the Ashton New Road route shortly before conversion in 1938. The trolleybus wires are already in position. *W. A. Camwell*

other traffic and it could also pull into the kerb at stops instead of halting in the middle of the road, while it also had the merits of being quiet, smooth running and free from fumes. On balance, though, it appeared to offer little advantage over the old-time tram, while it paled into insignificance beside the motorbus.

In Manchester's conditions, an important argument was the need to relieve congestion in the central areas of the city. This perennial problem was put forward as one of the prime reasons for the abandonment of the tramways. More than 20 years earlier, several committees had investigated this matter and produced their several reports; pointing to the processions of tramcars that made their way into and out of the city, they warned that saturation point was near and that only wider streets and a rapid transit system could provide a long-term solution. Neither of these measures had been adopted, and in the succeeding years the quantity of traffic had continued to increase. Now the only course was to adopt a mode of transport which had the utmost flexibility within the crowded confines of congested streets; this mode of transport

was the motorbus, unrestricted by wires or rails and able to mix freely with other traffic, so facilitating the general flow.

Manchester was also a special case because of the question of inter-running with other authorities. Through services between adjoining undertakings had a long history, but the disadvantages of the railbound tramcar had revealed the motorbus as the more suitable vehicle for such interurban services. The future obviously held the need for the maximum cooperation between the various operators, with the idea of a South East Lancashire Board still fresh in the mind even if it was not the most live issue. Difficulties could arise if one individual undertaking chose to operate trolleybuses while its neighbour opted for motorbuses; in such conditions the through running would call for duplication of vehicles, a wasteful and uneconomic procedure. And a glance around the Greater Manchester area showed that few of the undertakings were enthusiastic about trolleybuses; true, Manchester itself was satisfactorily interworking with Ashton, while the SLT was operating in conjunction with

Bolton, which was still hankering after its own trolley-bus system. But others, such as Rochdale, Oldham or the SHMD, even if they had powers for trolley vehicles, seemed to prefer the motorbus. There was no indication that a trolleybus network in any way comparable with the old tram network was likely to spring into existence. In the interests of coordination, the case for one type of vehicle was strong.

A comparison of operationg costs in Manchester again revealed the position peculiar to the city. The cost of operation per vehicle-mile was put at 14.087d for the motorbus, against 16.097d for the trolleybus; this difference of 2.010d per vehicle-mile added up to an annual total of more than £120,000 in favour of the bus. Among the components making up this figure, the cost of maintenance of the diesel engine was put at 2.446d per vehicle-mile, while the equivalent cost for a trolleybus was only 1.899d; however, the trolleybus required overhead equipment, and the cost of maintenance of this amounted to 0.53d per vehicle-mile, thus making the figure almost equal to that of the motorbus.

Working expenses and capital charges were affected by the mileage run per year by each vehicle, and here the trolleybus came out second best. The annual mileage obtained from trolleybuses at work in Manchester was stated at only 31,755 per vehicle, while the motorbus averaged 40,880 miles, the difference being accounted for by the lower operational speed of the trolleybuses on their routes compared with the overall operations of the bus network. The speed of the trolleybuses on the Ashton Old Road route was given as averaging 10.2mile/h against 10.9mile/h for buses

Not surprisingly, on capital cost the bus came out as the cheaper alternative. The cost of replacing the tramways by trolleybuses was estimated at £1,188,351, compared with only £855,800 if replacement was by motorbuses. The capital cost of vehicles was not too dissimilar; a four-wheel trolleybus cost £2,200 and a six-wheeler £2,560, while the motorbus was slightly cheaper at £2,000 for a four wheeler and £2,325 for a six-wheeler. However, the trolleybus of course required its overhead equipment; the cost of this where tramway overhead already existed was put at £3,232 per mile, while for new routes the cost would be £3,666 per mile. For the central area, where complicated junctions and layout would be needed, the cost would necessarily be higher.

Everything pointed to the cheaper alternative if the low level of fares was to be retained in the interests of the passenger. The need to keep fares as low as

120

possible had gained added importance with the programme of rehousing, whereby dwellers from the old inner areas were being relocated in new suburban estates where they incurred longer and more costly journeys to and from their work. The transport department was fulfilling a social need by keeping fares as low as possible. But if this policy was to continue, then it was essential that the cost of operation of any part of the system should not be increased to such an extent as to put it at risk. Hence future policy demanded the adoption of the most economical mode of transport. To add weight to this argument, it was pointed out that every instance of conversion from trams had resulted in an increase in revenue. The additional revenue on the Ashton Old Road route had been about the same as that obtained on other conversions; in the first six months the increase was 16.6%.

For the other side, the supporters of electric traction, whether tram or trolleybus, argued that it made use of home-produced fuel rather than imported oil. Moreover, it formed a valuable load for the generating capacity already installed in the city's electricity department, and this was urged in favour of continuing the use of electric transport in the shape of the trolleybus. Pilcher's report, however, while conceding that this was a factor, held that it should not be permitted to stand in the way of the adoption of the most economical means of transport. Every advantage should be taken of new technology to improve the economy of operations, even to the extent of reducing employment in the mining industry. It would be a retrograde step, he submitted, not to introduce new equipment, even if this meant that employment would thereby be reduced — an argument which has continued in Britain into the 1980s. As to the patriotic case for consuming home-produced fuel rather than imported, he claimed that it could equally be argued that it was instead more patriotic to run motorbuses using oil; since oil was heavily taxed, the more you used, the more money you were contributing to the national revenue!

Pilcher's report was approved by the transport committee on 23 August 1938 and subsequently by the finance committee on 29 August. Then on 7 September it was considered by the city council, which on a very close vote of 45 to 44 referred it for further investigation by a special sub-committee of the general and Parliamentary committee. In due course, on 1 February 1939 the city council again considered the transport committee's report, together with the reports of the Finance Committee and the special sub-committee. As a result of this exhaustive examination of the matter, the city council gave its approval (by no means unanimously: by 54 votes to 35) and also sanctioned an application for the loans that would be necessary to implement the proposals.

Examination by the special sub-committee of the general and parliamentary committee had resulted in a revision of some of the figures put forward in the trans-

Above left: One of Manchester's new trolleybuses, six-wheel Crossley No 1064, is delivered in March 1938. Note both trolleybus and tram overhead, while the tower wagon waits in attendance. *Leyland Motors, courtesy Ian Allan Library*

Right: Supporters of electric traction pleaded its more efficient use of home produced fuel, as well as its freedom from pollution; Bury Corporation bus and tram on the Radcliffe route. *W. A. Camwell*

port committee's report, which had apparently come out too favourably for the motorbus. The revision, however, did nothing to help the case for the trolley-bus. It was revealed, for example, that the mileage per vehicle per year was only 37,274 for the motorbus, and not 40,880 as previously reported; the trolleybus mileage was confirmed at 31,755. On the other hand it was found that the number of trolleybuses that would be required for a complete conversion had been under-stated; it was not 428 but 470 that would be needed, at an extra cost of £92,620. This revised the figure for the total cost of conversion to trolleybuses from the pre-vious estimate of £1,188,351 to £1,280,971; however, the cost of conversion to buses remained at a figure of £855,800, thus swinging the balance still further in the direction of the bus.

Further examination of the figures for operating costs showed that the position of the motorbus was not quite so favourable as had previously been presented. The basis of comparison was a 54-seat vehicle, whereas some of the trolleybuses were 68-seaters, which obviously had higher earning capacity, given sufficient traffic on their routes. Revi-sion of the figures put the cost per mile for a bus at 14.559d, an increase compared with the earlier figure of 14.087d, while the cost for the trolleybus was now put at 16.076d against 16.097d previously. Thus the difference is favour of the motorbus was reduced from 2.01d per mile to 1.517d. On this revised basis, therefore, the estimate of the saving in operating expenses (based on the total of 14.5million miles worked) in favour of the motorbus was reduced from £121,438 to only £85.305. Though the outcome was not so striking, the bus was still confirmed as the cheaper alternative.

Other points made in connection with the tramways illustrated the extent of the financial profit and loss —

mostly the latter. It was noted that the estimated loss on the tramways account for 1938-39 was £32,000, in addition to which an amount of £168,000 a year would have to be spent to undertake essential renewals and reconditionng if the trams were to be retained. As to the costs that would arise when the trams went, the report found that the cost of road reinstatement after the lifting of the tracks would be £660,537, of which £167,350 would be chargeable to the Transport Department while the remainder (almost £500,000) would fall on the rates. At the same time the finance committee would lose the sum of £11,155 a year in rates paid on permanent way and equipment, while the net annual loss of income to the electricity department would be £53,756.

The sub-committee rejected the suggestion that the result of all this would be to subsidise the transport department by putting these extra burdens on to the ratepayers. It pointed out, quite rightly, that for many years the transport department (and the tramways in particular) had in effect been subsidising both the highways and the electricity departments, which had both derived substantial benefits from the tramways, in the electricity load, the rates paid on the installations, and the road maintenance which had been borne by the trams, as well as the sums which had been passed over to the relief of rates. It was therefore time for the transport department to look to the interests of its passengers by operating the most economical form of transport in order to provide the lowest possible fares, regardless of the effects on other departments of the municipal economy. This argument illustrated not only the interdependence of the various parts of the municipal machinery, but also the underlying element of social benefit in the provision of local services.

Lingering doubts still troubled a few of the users. Some feared that buses would mean higher fares; while

Right: Could high-capacity trams be satisfactorily replaced by smaller buses? Bus proponents claimed they could, because of the greater flexibility of the bus. Trams appear to be outflanked by new buses in this 1938 scene in the centre of Bury. Tram No 9 dated from 1903 but had been extensively rebuilt as an 80-seater; the double-deck bus, a new Leyland Gearless Titan, is a 56-seater. *W. A. Camwell*

Above: One reason for Salford's rejection of the trolleybus was the need to use the same type of vehicle on through routes.
Salford tram No 224 waits at the Weaste terminus before starting its run to Deansgate, while a Corporation bus disappears into the distance. Weaste depot is on the right.   *W. A. Camwell*

Right: The end of an era: through the misty front window of a bus on a chill January day in 1949, a glimpse of Manchester's official 'Last Tram' as it makes its lonely final journey along Hyde Road, past Ardwick Green, to the depot. *Greater Manchester Transport, courtesy R. Dunning*

cheap workmen's fares had been retained on replacement buses, there was no legal obligation to provide such fares as there had been on the trams. Not everyone could afford to pay a little extra for a higher standard of service. And, in spite of efforts to prove the contrary, some people still believed the trams were better in fog. Then, how would the 56-seat buses cope with the loads handled by the 78-seat trams? 'Will I be among the unfortunates to be left behind in the rain?' Some were unhappy about the dependence on fuel oil; apart from the fact that electricity was generated from home-produced coal, it was also generated in the city's own power station. The loss of the trams would mean a loss of over £50,000 to the electricity department; would other consumers have to pay more to make up this loss? It was all very well to claim that transport should not have to subsidise other services, but would not the ratepayers in general have to make good the losses in rates and road maintenance charges?

Above: Last operator of tramcars in the Greater Manchester area was Stockport Corporation, where they survived until replaced by buses in 1951. Centre of the system was Mersey Square, seen here with No 80, a Craven-built car of the mid-1920s. *C. Carter*

Right: The postwar Manchester scene: against a background of the Cathedral, Corporation buses on the Altrincham route stand at their city terminus. Leading is No 4124, a Daimler CVG6 of 1950 with Metropolitan-Cammell 58-seat body. *G. H. F. Atkins*

There were other people to consider too; an instance of the effect of your next door neighbour's actions could be seen in Salford's decision just a month after the Manchester decision. On 1 March 1939 Salford City Council approved its transport committee's recommendation that the process of replacing its tramways by motorbuses should be continued. The committee came out against the adoption of trolley-buses; not only was the trolleybus less economical and less convenient in operation because of the difficulty of arranging a suitable terminus in the city centre, but it was essential for the adequate operation of through routes that Salford should use the same form of transport as its partners. In a word, if Manchester opted for the motorbus, then Salford had to do likewise.

And so the motorbus had triumphed. It had looked like a foregone conclusion for years. Manchester's trams seemed to have little to recommend them; confined to their tracks, they were blamed for contributing to traffic congestion, while the increasing speed and intensity of motor traffic made it more and more dangerous to have to go out into the middle of the street to board a car. Critics complained that they were noisy and slow, they had hard wooden seats, and their angularity, tinted glass and wrought ironwork made them a relic of Edwardian technology that had no place in the modern world of the 1930s. The buses on the other hand were new and fast; they had taken over the best and fastest services, they had comfortable upholstered seats, and they were smaller and less cold and cavernous. With their streamlined livery, they were the obvious contemporaries of the latest super-cinema. The transition from tram to bus appeared to be the most natural stage of evolution.

Once the fateful decision had been taken, things began to move quickly. Little more than a month later, Manchester Transport Committee was recommending the city council to accept contracts for the supply of 250 new buses and 77 trolleybuses, at a total cost of £643,600. The trolleybuses were to comprise the last of this type of vehicle that would be needed, but another 100 buses at a cost of £240,000 would still be required to complete the conversion programme. Accordingly in 1938 orders were placed for the 250 buses, divided almost equally between Crossley, Leyland and Daimler, while in 1939 the further 100 were also ordered, again divided equally between the three makers.

As it happened, world events conspired to ensure that the transformation was not to be as rapid as had been envisaged. Only a few months after the decision, the outbreak of World War 2 in September 1939 brought new problems. At this time Manchester still had well over 400 trams, many of which had to be kept going for a few more years than had been expected; indeed some had to be reinstated as bus services were curtailed.

In the light of the divergence of views over the use of electricity versus oil-powered transport, it was perhaps ironical that the war years should have brought practical lessons to add to the argument. Shortage of oil meant that many bus services had to be reduced, while trams were retained and trolleybuses were extended. Off-peak buses to Wythenshawe, for example, that showplace of the motor age, were cut back to the tram terminus at Princess Road, where once the tramways might have been extended on sleeper track as part of a rapid transit scheme. Other tram routes were reinstated along roads whence they had so recently been banished, while trolleybuses were extended along Rochdale Road to Conran Street and Moston, and to Denton and Haughton Green, basically on routes where only a few years earlier the trams had been displaced by motorbuses. At the end of the war there were still some 350 trams, while the trolleybus fleet had grown to about 150. It was not until 10 January 1949 that the last of Manchester's

trams were withdrawn, to complete the process which had begun on that famous Circular route nearly 20 years before.

In view of the prewar decision for the motorbus, it is interesting that in the early 1950s Manchester looked as though it might be set on a course of ambitious expansion of its trolleybus network. A critical examination of the comparative roles of the trolleybus and the diesel bus was contained in a report prepared in 1953 by the then general manager of the transport department, A. F. Neal. This set forth the advantages of the trolleybus on much the same basis as the prewar reports; it enjoyed a longer life and lower maintenance costs, it could have a larger carrying capacity, and it was smooth running, silent and free from fumes. On the other hand, compared with the diesel, it was a more expensive vehicle in first cost, and it required elaborate fixed equipment, while it was a less mobile vehicle in congested streets.

This last point, which reinforced the prewar case, proved to be crucial. The motorbus still had the overwhelming advantage of flexibility; partly this meant that it was able to negotiate junctions faster and that one bus was able to overtake another, thus facilitating traffic flow. More important was its flexibility in operation; it could easily be switched from one route to another according to the needs of traffic, while it was available to serve any route without being confined to fixed overhead. The report pointed out that many buses were used in the early morning to operate factory services, after which they quickly made their way (by short cuts or running non-stop) to suburban termini in time for the morning peak-hour commuter flow. It was estimated that an additional 80 vehicles

Left: Rochdale Corporation still favoured a streamlined livery for its new postwar vehicles; No 32 is an AEC Regent III with Weymann 56-seat body, delivered in 1947. *Ian Allan Library*

Above: Very similar to the 1939 styling was this Leyland PD2/1 Titan delivered to Stockport Corporation in 1949 as No 266. *Ian Allan Library*

would have been required if these services were worked by trolleybuses. Further, buses were used on limited-stop services between outer suburbs and city, and such working would not have been practicable with trolleybuses; a similar characteristic had helped to defeat the trams on the longer suburban and inter-urban routes.

Details of operating and power costs revealed a healthy position that would be grounds for gratification if it still obtained today! For trolleybuses, the operating cost per vehicle mile for a 60-seat four-wheeler was 28.775d, while revenue was 33.843d; for a 68-seat six-wheeler operating cost was 30.056d and revenue 35.480d. Thus, although the larger capacity six-wheeler had a higher operating cost, this was offset by its higher earning ability. Clearly the trolleybus was still a comfortably profitable mode of transport, though it is indicative of the postwar era of inflation that operating cost was already some 75% above the prewar level.

The crux of the comparison was shown in the figures of motive power cost. Because of the tax on fuel oil, the diesel bus was a more expensive vehicle to operate, but without the tax it was cheaper. Motive power costs per vehicle-mile for the diesel bus were put at 5.005d for fuel oil, of which the fuel itself accounted for only 1.573d and the tax for the remaining 3.452d, while for the trolleybus electrical energy cost 2.653d. It was an apparently contradictory national policy which ensured that the cheaper diesel bus was made artificially more expensive, thus encouraging the retention of the more costly trolleybus. The diesel also had the edge on other operating costs, and it was only the fuel tax which put it at a disadvantage, to the extent of giving the trolleybus a lead of 1.239d a mile.

Conclusive weight was added to the case by the fact that these figures applied only to existing trolleybus installations; the high cost of new fixed equipment ensured that any operational advantage on new routes could only have been very marginal at best. Moreover, the life of new overhead equipment could only have been justified by a long-term contract with the British Electricity Authority covering the cost of power. By this time the electricity generating industry had been nationalised, thus removing electricity supply from the ambit of the municipal economy with which it had been associated since the earliest days of the electric tramways. On the national scale, there was a shortage of generating capacity while the coal industry was struggling to meet the demand for coal; thus the possible trend of electricity costs was not conducive to a commitment to the trolleybus.

The message of the report was clear: there could be no swing to the trolleybus. Economic conditions and the outlook for fuel supplies were such that no adequate justification could be made for the large-scale adoption of the electric vehicle, a situation which was reflected in the gradual decline and eventual demise of the trolleybus throughout Britain. As far as Manchester was concerned, the report was sufficient to lead to the purchase of a new batch of BUTs to replace old vehicles to serve existing routes, but its conclusion confirmed the decision taken 15 years previously: there could be no return to electric traction in Manchester's streets.

Below: This 8ft wide Daimler CVG6 with 54-seat Metropolitan-Cammell body was delivered to Salford City Transport as No 351 in 1950. *Ian Allan Library*

The Manchester bus in the early postwar period:
Right: No 3280, a Leyland Titan PD2/3 of 1950;
Below right: No 4494, a Daimler CVG5 of 1955 with MCW Orion body. *G. H. F. Atkins*

GOLDEN STREAM TEA
62
ALBERT Sq
3280
JND 681

12
OLD TRAFFORD
STRETFORD
URMSTON
FLIXTON
Crown WALLPAPERS say welcome!
MOTHER'S
PRIDE
BREAD
4494
PND 494

The non-existent board

' It is desirable that all the means of transportation should be concentrated under one management. '
J. M. McElroy, General Manager,
Manchester Corporation Tramways, 1914

Paradoxically the growth of municipal enterprise, with its strong sense of corporate identity, served to emphasise the fact that transport operations could not be constrained by local boundaries. This was especially significant in the Greater Manchester region, where individual towns, many with their own transport undertakings, coalesced to form a conurbation; through working and joint services became an essential feature. Expansion of the residential area with the rise of the motorbus, bringing more longer-distance travel, together with the intensification of congestion and the resultant schemes for rapid transit and railway electrification, further strengthened the case for wider coordination, possibly under some kind of overall regional authority.

Even at the height of municipal enthusiasm the idea that some form of joint body should coordinate the working of the various undertakings in the area was being aired. Back in 1902 Salford had proposed the formation of a joint board (perhaps on the lines of the then-new SHMD Board) to run the tramways of both Salford and Manchester, and to include members from the local authorities on whose behalf the corporations carried out operations in their respective districts. The plan was opposed by Manchester, which was busy

Below: The complexities of municipal transport are exemplified in this view outside Radcliffe Council Buildings. Though Radcliffe owned its own tram tracks, the services were provided by neighbouring Bury Corporation, one of whose cars is seen reversing for the return journey to its home town.   *W. A. Camwell*

extending its own municipal system, and the proposition never materialised. Salford tried again in 1929, when it promoted a Bill to set up a Tramways and Omnibus Board for South East Lancashire, but this time the proposal was blocked by Parliament.

In 1914 Manchester's tramways manager had urged the need for an overall authority embracing all transport in the Greater Manchester area, but it was not until the 1930s that serious and lengthy discussions towards the creation of a joint transport body looked as though they might end in the establishment of a new pattern. However, the innumerable meetings and talks reached no obvious practical conclusion, and it was left to the 1960s to produce the passenger transport authorities.

By the 1930s a new and significant factor influenced the thinking behind the need for a joint body. This was the motorbus, which had greatly increased in numbers and in its share of the traffic; and, while the municipalities were now themselves deeply committed to bus operation, they were not the only ones in the field. Companies such as the North Western Road Car Company, Lancashire United Transport and Ribble, together with the independent operators who had flourished during the 1920s, had shown the necessity for some means of control in an area where municipal and company interests might overlap.

Further, under the Road Traffic Act of 1930, the licensing of bus services had been taken out of the hands of local authorities and placed with the newly-established Area Traffic Commissioners, who were free to dispense licences as they thought fit. Thus the local authorities even though they were given wider powers to run their own buses, no longer had control (ineffective though it may sometimes have been) over outside bus operators who might enter their territory and take traffic away from their own services. Co-ordination seemed preferable to competition. In 1931 the Transport Minister, Herbert Morrison, had warned that if the municipal operators did not cooperate, 'taking the big view of the transport problem instead of the parish pump view', they would be beaten at the job by private enterprise. The motorbus was tending towards the breakdown of local barriers.

In the same year, at the instigation of Oldham, a conference was called to discuss a proposal for the amalgamation of the municipal transport undertakings in the Manchester area and the establishment of a form of central control. Such a municipal transport board or regional board would aim to include all interests in the area, and it was hoped that the large company operators (notably Lancashire United, North Western and Ribble) would participate. In putting forward the proposition, Oldham argued that under existing conditions transport developments could not be looked at simply within the confines of a municipal boundary; the time had come when local authorities should co-operate with one another and with other operators, instead of 'dissipating their resources in bitter struggles' among themselves.

A conference was duly held, attended by representatives from Manchester, Salford, Oldham, Rochdale, Bury, Ashton, Bolton, Stockport, the SHMD, Wigan and Leigh, and in a flush of enthusiasm a report was drafted setting out the advantages and disadvanatges of such a plan. Among the advantages to be gained were the possibility of establishing more through routes among the various participants; a more economical use of vehicles, since they could be switched from one operator to another as the need arose; economy in the overhaul and maintenance of vehicles with central control; and the reduction of administrative costs with centralisation and the elimination of the work involved in the running of joint services. The big disadvantage was the possibility of over-centralisation, which could take away local initiative and lead to an inflexible structure. Nevertheless, an outline organisation was worked out to enable local operations to be controlled at local level.

The year 1933 saw the creation of the London Passenger Transport Board, which was just the sort of organisation that was in the minds of the Manchester area proponents. If it could be done in London, why not in Manchester? The LPTB was a unification of the various transport undertakings in the capital, with the aim of creating a coordinated system and eliminating wasteful competition. With this shining example before them, the Lancashire representatives bent to their task with renewed vigour.

Accordingly, in 1933 a proposal for a joint board for South Lancashire, covering an area of about 21 miles by 15, was put to Manchester, Salford, Bury, Oldham, Rochdale, Bolton, Stockport and the SHMD. It was proposed that a Parliamentary Bill should be promoted to allow for the merger of the transport undertakings of the local authorities and the resultant creation of an area board. Negotiations proceeded, and early in 1934 Manchester City Council approved in principle the formation of a 'Joint Municipal Transport Board for South East Lancashire and East Cheshire' and appointed representatives to attend a conference on the subject.

Cracks in the solidarity soon became apparent. Wigan and Leigh were ruled out, in that their own services did not work in close conjunction with other operators. Then Bury and Stockport decided to withdraw. Stockport claimed that such a merger might oblige it to change over to buses and eliminate its profitable trams, with serious effects on its electricity department and the borough's rates; moreover, Stockport saw its future in expansion southward into Cheshire rather than northward into Manchester.

Operations of the three principal bus companies would have been brought within the ambit of an area scheme; representing their fleets in the early 1950s are:
Above left: A Lancashire United Guy Arab with Weymann body at Salford bus station on a service to Bolton;
Below left: Ribble Motor Services' Leyland Titans (with respectively East Lancs and Burlingham bodies) in Manchester Lower Mosley Street bus station on service to Clitheroe;
Above: North Western Road Car Company Bristol as rebodied by Willowbrook, in Manchester Piccadilly on service to Wilmslow and Alderley. *All: G. H. F. Atkins*

In 1935 both Bolton and the SHMD decided not to go any further, while Ashton also had second thoughts. Thus by the time of the meeting at which a final decision was expected to be taken, only four of the original participants remained: Manchester, Salford, Oldham and Rochdale. However, to redress the balance, the two main line railway companies, the LMS and LNER, agreed to take part; at which Oldham said that, in that case, it too would withdraw.

Differences seem to have been patched up, though, and at last the conference in early 1937 was attended by all the original participants, together with representatives of the LUT, North Western and Ribble, as well as the LMS and the LNER. It was agreed that the proposal for a joint board should be submitted to a special sub-committee which should be asked to prepare a report. This sub-committee consequently reported that there was a case for investigating the possibility of such an organisation, including cooperation with the railways, but it did not recommend that the matter should be further pursued at that time.

One of the strong supporters of amalgamation was Manchester transport manager, Stuart Pilcher, who questioned whether 'the existing local authorities' transport areas with their limited spheres of influence are now suitable for the provision of road passenger transport on the most economical and efficient lines'. Urging the economies of scale that could be achieved by a unified organisation, he stressed the 'possibility of economy to be achieved by the merger of undertakings whose sphere of control is too small in the light of modern ideas'.

Factors which no doubt influenced the thinking on a new form of organisation included the high degree of

Above: The proposed area board would have ended the intermingling of different operators' vehicles, such as this scene in Stockport's Mersey Square. A Stockport Corporation car on the left works a local town service, while the Manchester Corporation car on the right runs on the Stockport-Manchester route.   *W. A. Camwell*

coordination already in existence among the various bodies, both local authorities and companies. Admittedly the idea of bringing the railways into some kind of joint board, of the type that had been set up across the Pennines in Sheffield and Halifax and had been proposed for the Manchester area some time before, had foundered, thereby ruling out the possibility of full road and rail coordination. Nevertheless, co-ordination of bus services had been brought to a fine art on the basis of a long tradition; it was now especially valuable when most of the local authorities concerned had decided to change over from trams to buses, so further facilitating the provision of integrated services.

Neither had the activities of the licensing authority proved so detrimental to the municipalities. On the contrary, far from provoking competition with municipal operators, the 1930 Act had served to stabilise the industry, so that licensing restrictions were severely applied. The local authorities had come out well, with little fear of unrestricted competition to their services, while on the other hand the Traffic Commissioners had encouraged rationalisation and cooperation.

Above all, in noting the fate of the proposed area board, in cannot be overlooked that municipal pride was a factor to be reckoned with. The local authorities over the course of years had built up their own transport undertakings, generated pride in them, and based them on a policy of social service, with cheap fares and generous facilities to meet the needs of their own citizens. They could not be expected to look

enthusiastically at the idea that their services should be taken under the control of a large and possibly remote organisation which might not be so attuned to the requirements of their individual locality. Pilcher recognised that the great problem was the fear of the 'loss of local identity'. and although he suggested this might be overcome by the retention of local committees for local purposes, the corporate coat of arms on the town's buses was still a symbol of pride.

Nothing had materialised before World War 2 came along to overshadow such problems for the next few years, but the postwar period saw it again surfacing intermittently in various forms. The Transport Act of 1947, which included the nationalisation of the railways and London Transport, also provided for the establishment of area schemes for passenger transport operation, and Manchester would doubtless have been the centre of one of these schemes. However, this provision never took effect and it was repealed under the Transport Act of 1953. In 1966 more discussion took place in Manchester on the possibility of an area or regional system of bus services; the participants included the local authorities of Ashton, Bolton, Bury, Leigh, Manchester, Oldham, Ramsbottom, Rochdale, Salford, Stockport and the SHMD, as well as Lancashire United, North Western and Ribble. Following the talks, a steering committee was appointed.

But before much longer the Transport Act of 1968 provided for the establishment of passenger transport authorities in the main conurbations, with the object of taking over the various undertakings in those areas and coordinating both road and rail services by means of passenger transport executives. One of these bodies was set up for South East Lancashire and North East Cheshire (SELNEC) in 1969, to be succeeded by the Greater Manchester Passenger Transport Executive under the new Greater Manchester Metropolitan County created by the Local Government Act of 1972. Thus the idea of an area authority had at last become a reality and a new era in regional transport had begun.

Conclusion

'The function of a municipal transport authority is not necessarily that of making large profits. The main purpose is to provide a satisfactory service to the public at the lowest possible price.'

C. P. Paige, General Manager,
Oldham Corporation Transport, 1944

If any period can be called the 'Golden Age' of urban transport it must surely be the first half of the 20th century. At its start the electric tramway was revolutionising town travel habits, while by its close the replacing bus network maintained a crucial part in the regional economy before it had to face the full onslaught of the private car. In the years between, cheap mass transport facilities enhanced the quality of daily life; ordinary people were enabled to seek a wider choice of employment, to move out of overcrowded central housing into new suburbs, and to enjoy easy access to entertainment and recreation

In the Greater Manchester region, a tradition of municipal service flourished. Local authorities developed undertakings of strong individuality — to the delight of the enthusiast, who revelled in the variety of vehicles and liveries, but to the despair of the tidy-minded rationalist who saw the multifarious scene as a cauldron of petty jealousies and inefficiencies. Certainly the much discussed Area Board never came into being during this period, but coordination of services was widely practised by both municipalities and companies. How far the existence of a multitude of operators resulted in increased working costs, and how far the insistence of each on its separate identity deferred integration, are questions that can only be suggested, though the experience of the Greater Manchester PTE indicates something of the answers.

No less difficult to assess are the benefits conferred

Below: A hint of what might have been a common scene in Bolton if the corporation's plans for trolleybuses had reached fruition. A South Lancashire vehicle, one of the company's postwar Weymann-bodied Sunbeams, stands at the Bolton terminus of the route to Leigh.
R. Brook

Left: By the middle of the 1930s the double-deck bus had assumed the shape it was to retain for the next 25 years: typical was the style of this Stockport Corporation Leyland Gearless Titan seen in Piccadilly in 1935. *G. H. F. Atkins*

by municipal ownership. The corporate tradition emphasised the social service role of local transport; profitability was not the only — or necessarily the primary — criterion of success. Rather, the supply of cheap and plentiful local transport was regarded as being of equal importance to the wellbeing of the town-dweller as the supply of electricity, gas or water. As Manchester's tramways manager J. M. McElroy had expressed it as far back as 1906, the main object was 'to give the people the most efficient and expeditious means of locomotion at the cheapest cost to themselves'. In a later age of declining services, we have been forced to rediscover the social role of transport.

Nor was it practicable to isolate the transport department from other areas of the municipal economy. When the fate of the Manchester trams was hanging in the balance, their relationship to other elements of civic policy was pleaded in their support; they offered extra-cheap fares to assist those who had moved to the new council estates, they contributed substantially to road maintenance and to the relief of rates, and by providing a useful load to the corporation's electricity department they helped to keep power charges down for other consumers. Transport was integrated into the local pattern; it could not be considered in isolation.

'Golden Age' this may have been, but it was not without its problems. Hindsight may point to the missed opportunities of the past: to the rapid transit lines and subways discussed in the heyday of the tramways, to the proposals for railway electrification in the 1920s, to the sleeper track tramways which could have formed the nucleus of a light rail transit system, to the underground that never was, and to the area board envisaged in the 1930s. It might all have been so different. But, as we are aware in our own age, transport is circumscribed by the conditions of its time: by restraints on capital expenditure, by limitations of costs, by competition and integration, by adaptation to new modes of transport, as well as by external factors such as population redistribution, trade depression and world wars. It is therefore the achievements that are deserving of recall and it is hoped that this book may have served to remind us of some of those achievements, while at the same time awakening memories of Greater Manchester's transport as it was.

The Growth of Municipal Transport in Greater Manchester

	Number of trams at maximum	Number of buses in 1953
Ashton	40	74*
Bolton	162	285
Bury	60	97
Leigh	—	61
Manchester	952	1,500†
Oldham	150	240
Ramsbottom	—	19
Rochdale	94	155
Salford	230	324
SHMD	64	81
Stockport	85	168
Wigan	92	162
Total:	1,929	3,166

*Includes 24 trolleybuses
†Includes 193 trolleybuses

136

Chronology

1754		'Flying Coach': Manchester to London in $4\frac{1}{2}$ days
1757		Sankey Canal
1760		Manchester to London 3-day coach
1761	17 July	Bridgewater Canal opened
1767		Manchester-Liverpool coach
1777		Pickford's 'Flying Wagon': Manchester to London in $4\frac{1}{2}$ days
1785	25 July	Leeds-Manchester-Liverpool Mail Coach starts
1804	21 December	Rochdale Canal opened
1824	1 January	John Greenwood starts Manchester-Pendleton coach service
1824		Manchester to London coach in 24 hours
1828	1 August	Bolton & Leigh Railway opened
1830	15 September	Liverpool & Manchester Railway opened
1830		Manchester-Stockport horse bus starts
1833		Manchester-London *Telegraph* coach: 18 hours
1837	4 July	Grand Junction Railway opened
1838	29 May	Manchester & Bolton Railway opened
1839	4 July	Manchester-Littleborough railway opened
1840	4 June	Manchester-Stockport railway opened
1841	1 March	Manchester & Leeds Railway opened
1841	17 November	Manchester-Godley railway opened
1842	10 May	London Road station, Manchester, opened
1842	10 August	Manchester-Stockport-Crewe railway opened
1842	10 December	Railway extended from Godley to Broadbottom (Mottram)
1844	1 May	Manchester, Hunts Bank station (Victoria) opened
1844	8 August	Railway extended to Hadfield and Woodhead
1845	9 June	Glossop branch opened
1845	22 December	Formal opening of Manchester-Sheffield railway (opened to public on 23 December)
1845	23 December	Stalybridge branch opened
1849	20 July	Manchester South Junction & Altrincham Railway opened
1857	1 August	GNR starts Manchester-London service
1865	1 March	Manchester Carriage Company established
1877	17 May	First tramway in Manchester
1877	9 July	Manchester Central station opened
1880	7 May	Manchester-Stockport tram service starts
1880	1 July	New Manchester Central station opened
1880	31 July	First tramway in Wigan
1880	1 September	First tramway in Bolton
1882	27 July	First tramway in Rochdale
1882	6 November	Holcombe Brook branch opened
1883	12 March	First part of Manchester, Bury, Rochdale and Oldham Company steam tramways opened
1884	1 May	New Manchester Victoria station opened
1890	4 April	Stockport and Hazel Grove tramway opened
1894	1 January	Manchester Ship Canal opened for traffic (formal opening by Queen Victoria: 21 May)
1897	23 July	Trafford Park gas trams start operation
1899	15 March	Great Central Railway starts Manchester-London service

1899	12 June	Oldham Ashton & Hyde electric tramways start
1899	9 December	First electric tramways in Bolton
1900	2 January	Last horse trams in Bolton
1900	6 August	South Lancashire Tramways Company incorporated
1900	15 December	First electric tramways in Oldham
1901	25 January	First electric tramways in Wigan
1901	6 June	First Manchester Corporation electric tramways
1901	26 August	Stockport Corporation electric tramways start
1901	4 October	Salford Corporation tramways opened
1902	27 March	Middleton electric tramways opened
1902	22 May	Rochdale Corporation tramways start
1902	1 June	Manchester-Stockport electric tram service starts
1902	16 August	Ashton-under-Lyne Corporation tramways opened
1902	20 October	First section of SLT tramways opened
1903	31 March	Last horse trams in Manchester
1903	3 June	Bury Corporation tramways opened
1903	14 July	Trafford Park electric tramways start operation
1904	1 March	LNWR 'Sunny South Special' starts: Manchester-South Coast
1904	21 May	SHMD Board tramways opened
1905	5 July	Stockport-Hazel Grove electric tramway starts
1905	20 September	Last steam trams (Heywood Corporation)
1905	29 December	Lancashire United Tramways established
1906	23 March	First LUT motorbus services
1906	1 May	Oldham-Rochdale joint tram service started
1907	21 January	Through tram service Manchester-Oldham inaugurated
1907	20 May	Bolton-Bury through tram service started
1908	1 May	Last Trafford Park gas trams
1909	8 February	LNWR Manchester-Styal-Wilmslow line opened
1909	1 May	Passenger services started on Manchester-Styal-Wilmslow line
1909	14 June	Bolton-SLT through tram services started
1909	1 August	Joint tram service Rochdale-Bury started
1910	8 August	Mayfield station, Manchester, brought into use
1913	10 March	Stockport Corporation trolleybuses started
1913	12 May	Oldham Corporation's first motorbuses
1913	29 July	Bury-Holcombe Brook electric train service started
1913	14 August	Ramsbottom trolleybuses started
1916	17 April	Manchester-Bury electric train service opened
1918	29 March	Bury-Holcombe Brook electric train service resumed after conversion from overhead to third-rail
1919	24 May	Manchester-Southport-Blackpool air service started (until 2 September)

Below: Manchester's effective people-mover: the big bogie tramcar. No 492 was one of some 350 new cars put into service by Manchester Corporation during the 1920s when the city's tramways were still expanding. *W. A. Camwell*

1919	9 June	First Wigan Corporation motorbus service
1919	8 October	First Stockport Corporation motorbuses
1920	5 July	First Salford Corporation motorbuses
1920	11 September	Stockport trolleybuses end
1921	4 March	First Salford Corporation motorbus service into Manchester
1921	2 July	Oldham Ashton & Hyde tramways taken over by Ashton, Manchester and SHMD
1922	23 October	Manchester-London air service started
1923	23 April	North Western Road Car Company formed
1923	29 December	Bolton Corporation re-starts motorbus services
1925	7 May	Wigan Corporation starts trolleybuses
1925	9 August	Middleton tramways taken over by Manchester, Rochdale and Oldham
1925	8 August	Manchester-Rochdale through joint tram service started
1925	26 August	Ashton-Oldham joint trolleybus service started
1926	17 March	Rochdale Corporation starts motorbus service
1926	5 September	Ashton-Oldham trolleybus service ended
1926	18 November	Through joint bus service Bury-Ramsbottom
1927	11 April	Manchester Limited Stop bus service started (Manchester-Gatley)
1929	2 August	Midland Red and North Western start Manchester-London coach service
1930	6 April	Last trams on Manchester's 53 route
1930	3 August	SLT starts trolleybus operation
1930	13 December	Manchester's first diesel-engined bus in service
1931	28 March	Last Wigan trams
1931	31 March	Ramsbottom trolleybuses cease
1931	11 May	Electric services started on Manchester, South Junction & Altrincham Railway
1931	30 September	Last Wigan trolleybuses
1932	12 November	Last Rochdale Corporation trams
1933	17 December	SLT Bolton-Leigh trolleybus service started
1934	22 January	Bolton-Bury joint bus service replaces trams
1938	1 March	First Manchester trolleybus services started
1938	1 March	Last Ashton Corporation trams
1938	25 June	Manchester Ringway airport opened
1945	12 May	Last tram service on SHMD
1946	3 August	Last Oldham Corporation tram service
1947	29 March	Last Bolton Corporation trams
1947	31 March	Last Salford Corporation trams
1949	10 January	Last Manchester Corporation trams
1949	13 February	Last Bury Corporation trams
1951	25 March	Bury-Holcombe Brook electric trains replaced by steam trains
1951	25 August	Last Stockport Corporation trams
1952	7 May	Bury-Holcombe Brook line closed
1954	14 June	Manchester-Glossop electric train service started
1954	14 September	Manchester-Sheffield electric train services inaugurated
1958	31 August	SLT ends trolleybus operation
1958	4 December	New Piccadilly, Manchester, bus station opened
1960	28 August	Mayfield station, Manchester, closed to passengers
1960	12 September	Manchester-Crewe electric services started
1966	30 December	Last Manchester and Ashton trolleybuses
1969	1 November	SELNEC PTA takes over municipal transport in Ashton, Bolton, Bury, Leigh, Manchester, Oldham, Ramsbottom, Rochdale, Salford, SHMD, Stockport
1974	1 April	SELNEC becomes Greater Manchester Transport
1976	1 February	LUT taken over by Greater Manchester Transport

Bibliography

General

Briggs, Asa; *Victorian Cities*; Odhams, 1963.

British Association; *Manchester and Its Region*, a survey prepared for the British Association meeting in Manchester 1962; Manchester University Press, 1962.

Frangopulo, N. J.; *Tradition in Action: the Historical Evolution of the Greater Manchester County*; E. P. Publishing, 1977.

Freeman, T. W.; *Lancashire, Cheshire and the Isle of Man*; Nelson, 1966.

Manchester Corporation; *Transport Diamond Jubilee*; 1961.

McKay, John P.; *Tramways and Trolleys: the Rise of Urban Mass Transport in Europe*; Princeton University Press, 1976.

Transport History

Bett, W. H., and Gillham, J. C., edited Price, J. H.; *The Tramways of South East Lancashire*; Light Railway Transport League, 1976.

Body, A. H.; *It Happened Round Greater Manchester: Canals and Waterways*; Greater Manchester Council, 1975.

Clarke, John; *It Happened Round Greater Manchester: Railways*; Greater Manchester Council, 1976.

Eyre, D. M., Heaps, C. W., Taylor, C.; *Manchester's Trolleybuses*; Manchester Transport Museum Society, 1968.

Forbes, N. N., Felton, B. J., Rush, R. W.; *The Electric Lines of the Lancashire & Yorkshire Railway*; Electric Railway Society, 1976.

Gilbert, A. C., Knight, N. R.; *Railways Around Manchester*; Manchester Transport Museum Society, 1973.

Gray, Edward; *The Tramways of Salford*; Manchester Transport Museum Society, 1967.

Gray, Edward; *Trafford Park Tramways*; Oakwood Press, 1964.

Gray, Edward; *The Manchester Carriage and Tramways Company*; Manchester Transport Museum Society, 1977.

Kirby, A. K.; *Dan Boyle's Railway — a Record of Manchester Corporation Tramways 1901-1906*; Manchester Transport Museum Society, 1974.

Kirby, A. K.; *Middleton Tramways*; Manchester Transport Museum Society, 1976.

Kirby, A. K.; *Manchester's Little Tram*; Manchester Transport Museum Society, 1979.

Hyde, W. G. S.; *The Manchester Bury Rochdale and Oldham Steam Tramway*; Transport Publishing Company, 1979.

Marshall, Maurice; *Stockport Corporation Tramways*; Manchester Transport Museum Society, 1975.

Mason, Eric; *The Lancashire & Yorkshire Railway in the Twentieth Century*; Ian Allan Ltd, 1954.

Owen, David; *Canals to Manchester*; Manchester University Press, 1977.

Rochdale Canal; Waterways Handbooks, 1975.

Stretch, E. K.; *The Tramways of Wigan*; Manchester Transport Museum Society, 1978.

Yearsley, Ian; *The Manchester Tram*; Advertiser Press, 1962.

Periodicals

Buses; Modern Transport; Omnibus Magazine; The Railway Magazine; Tramway and Railway World (later Transport World); Tramway Review.

Index

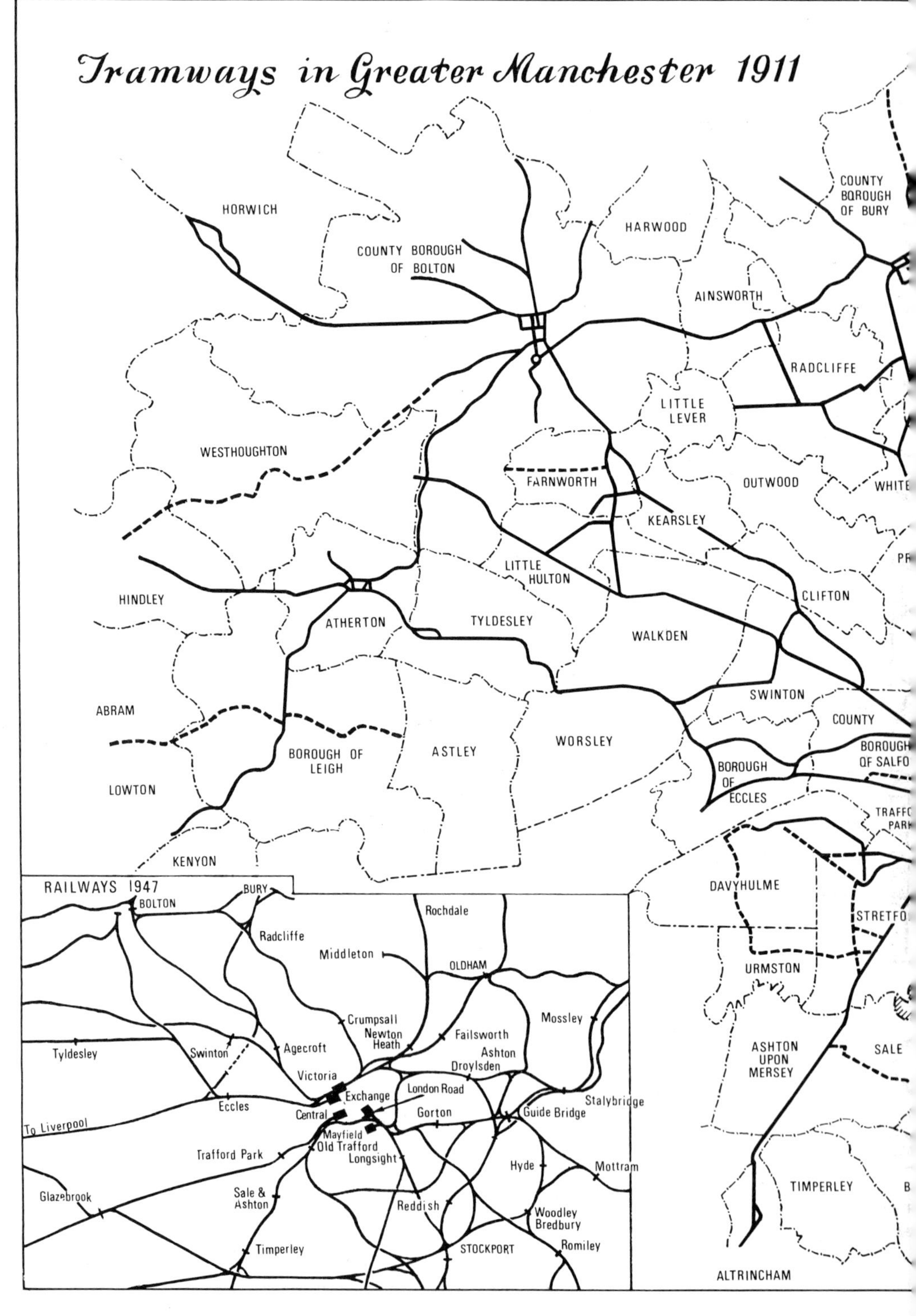

Tramways in Greater Manchester 1911
HORWICH
COUNTY BOROUGH OF BOLTON
HARWOOD
COUNTY BOROUGH OF BURY
AINSWORTH
RADCLIFFE
LITTLE LEVER
WESTHOUGHTON
FARNWORTH
OUTWOOD
WHITE
KEARSLEY
PR
HINDLEY
LITTLE HULTON
CLIFTON
ATHERTON
TYLDESLEY
WALKDEN
ABRAM
SWINTON
COUNTY
WORSLEY
BOROUGH OF SALFO
ASTLEY
BOROUGH OF LEIGH
BOROUGH OF ECCLES
LOWTON
TRAFFO PAR
KENYON
DAVYHULME
RAILWAYS 1947
BURY
STRETFO
BOLTON
Rochdale
Radcliffe
URMSTON
Middleton
OLDHAM
ASHTON UPON MERSEY
SALE
Crumpsall
Mossley
Newton Heath
Failsworth
Tyldesley
Swinton
Agecroft
Ashton
Droylsden
Victoria
To Liverpool
Eccles
Exchange
London Road
Central
Gorton
Guide Bridge
Stalybridge
Mayfield
Old Trafford
Trafford Park
Longsight
Hyde
Mottram
Glazebrook
Sale & Ashton
TIMPERLEY
B
Woodley
Reddish
Bredbury
Timperley
STOCKPORT
Romiley
ALTRINCHAM